NOVEMBER 50 COLORING PAGES FOR OLDER KIDS RELAXATION

SHIH CHIEN HUA

PUBLISHED BY:
SHIH CHIEN HUA
Copyright © 2018

SEABIRD SHOP >50FOR

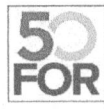

FB FAN PAGE

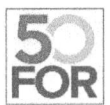

Disclaimer
The information contained in this book is for general information purposes only. The information is provided by the authors and while we endeavor to keep the information up to date and correct, we make no representations or warranties of any kind, express or implied, about the completeness, accuracy, reliability, suitability or availability with respect to the book or the information, products, services, or related graphics contained in the book for any purpose. Any reliance you place on such information is therefore strictly at your own risk.

NOVEMBER 1ST

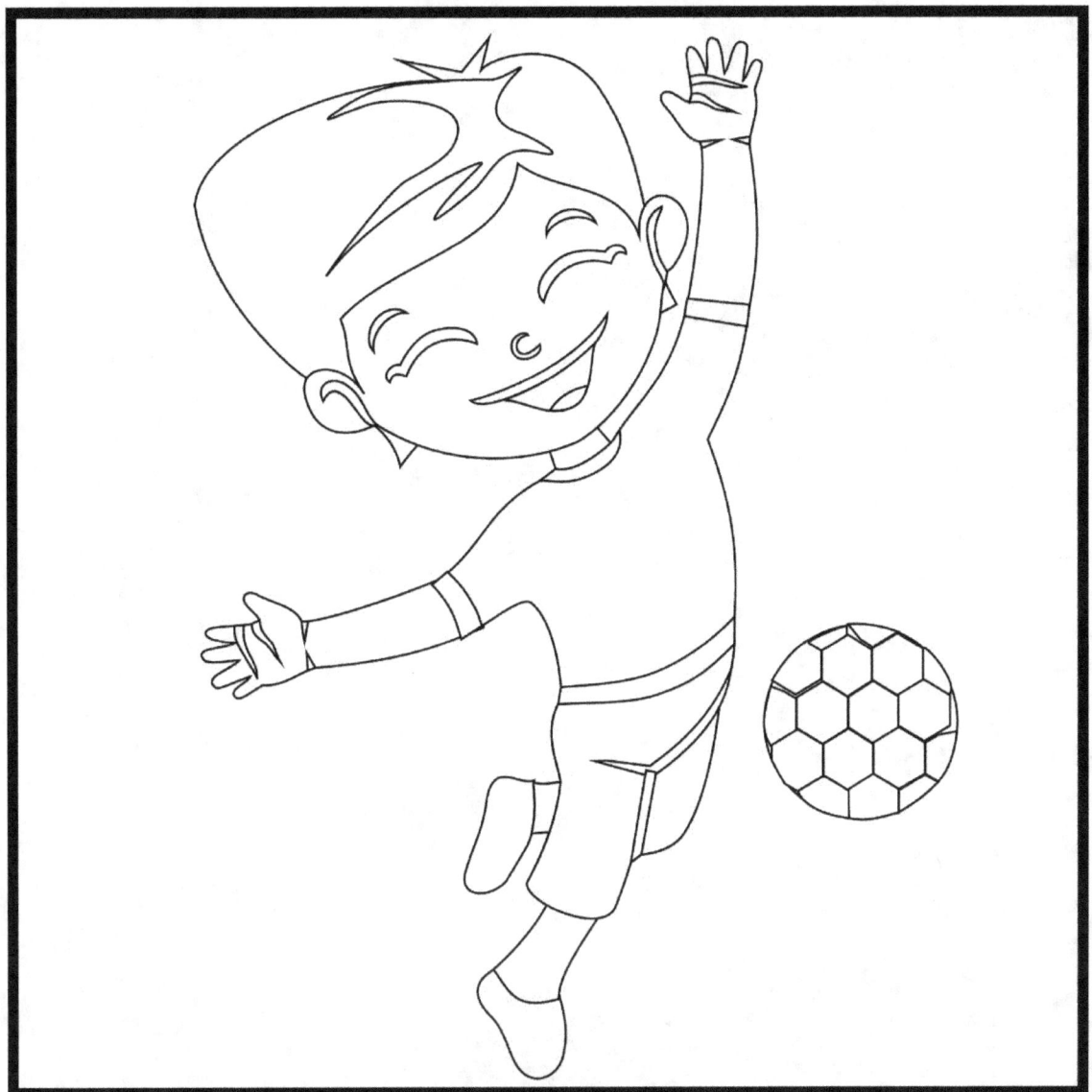

note:

_____

_____

_____

NOVEMBER 2ND

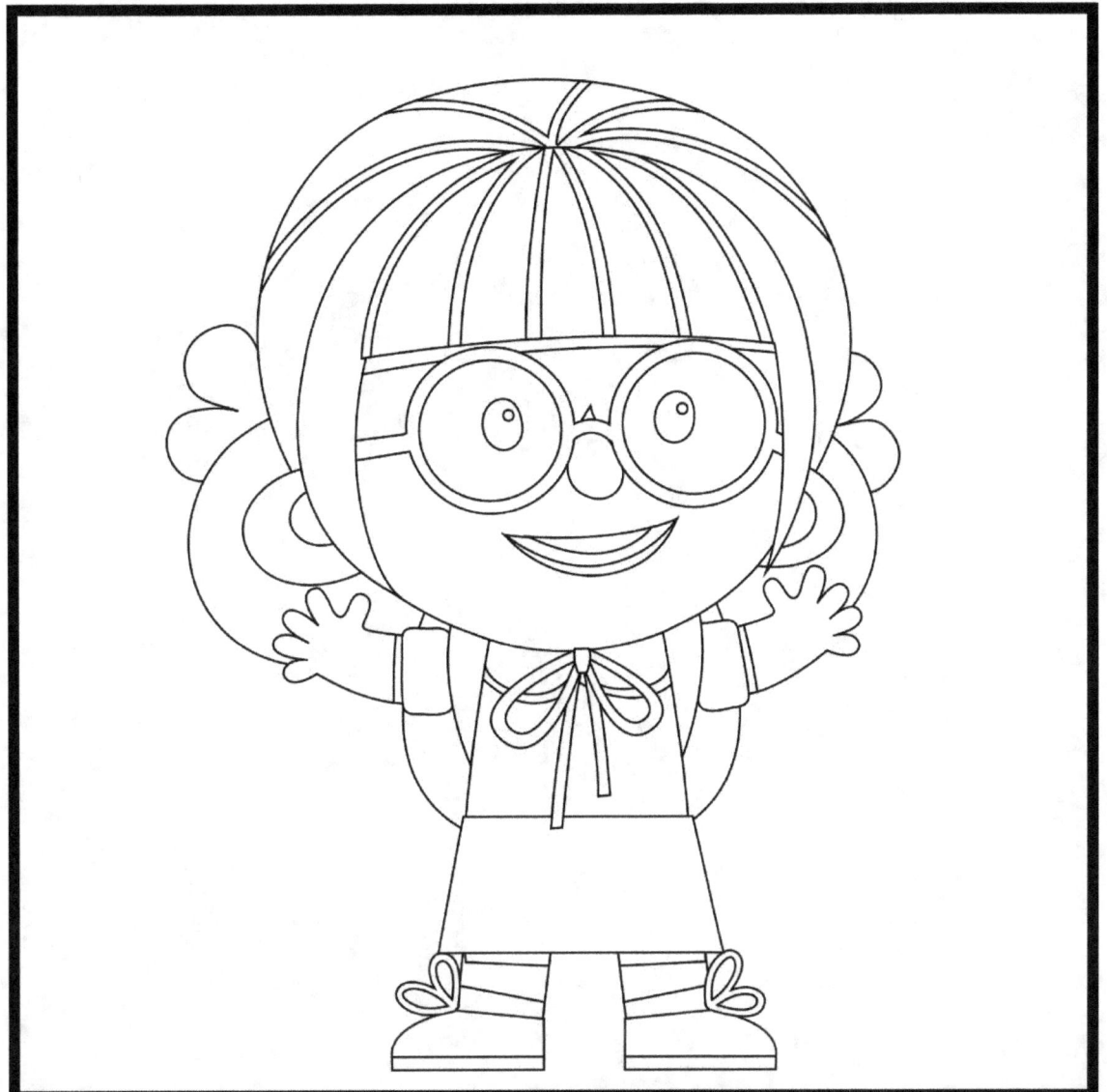

note:

_____

_____

_____

NOVEMBER 3RD

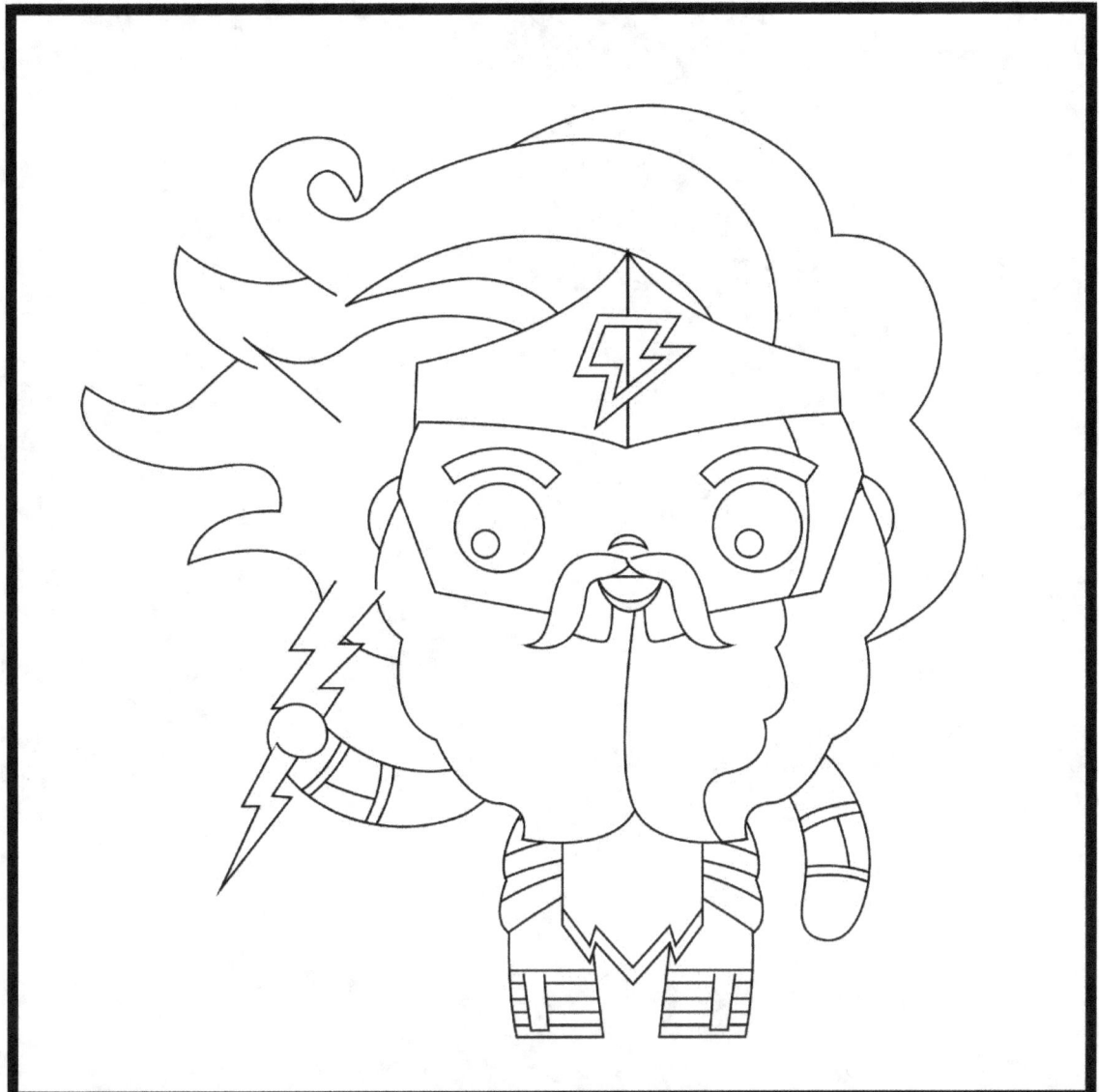

note:

_____

_____

_____

NOVEMBER 4TH

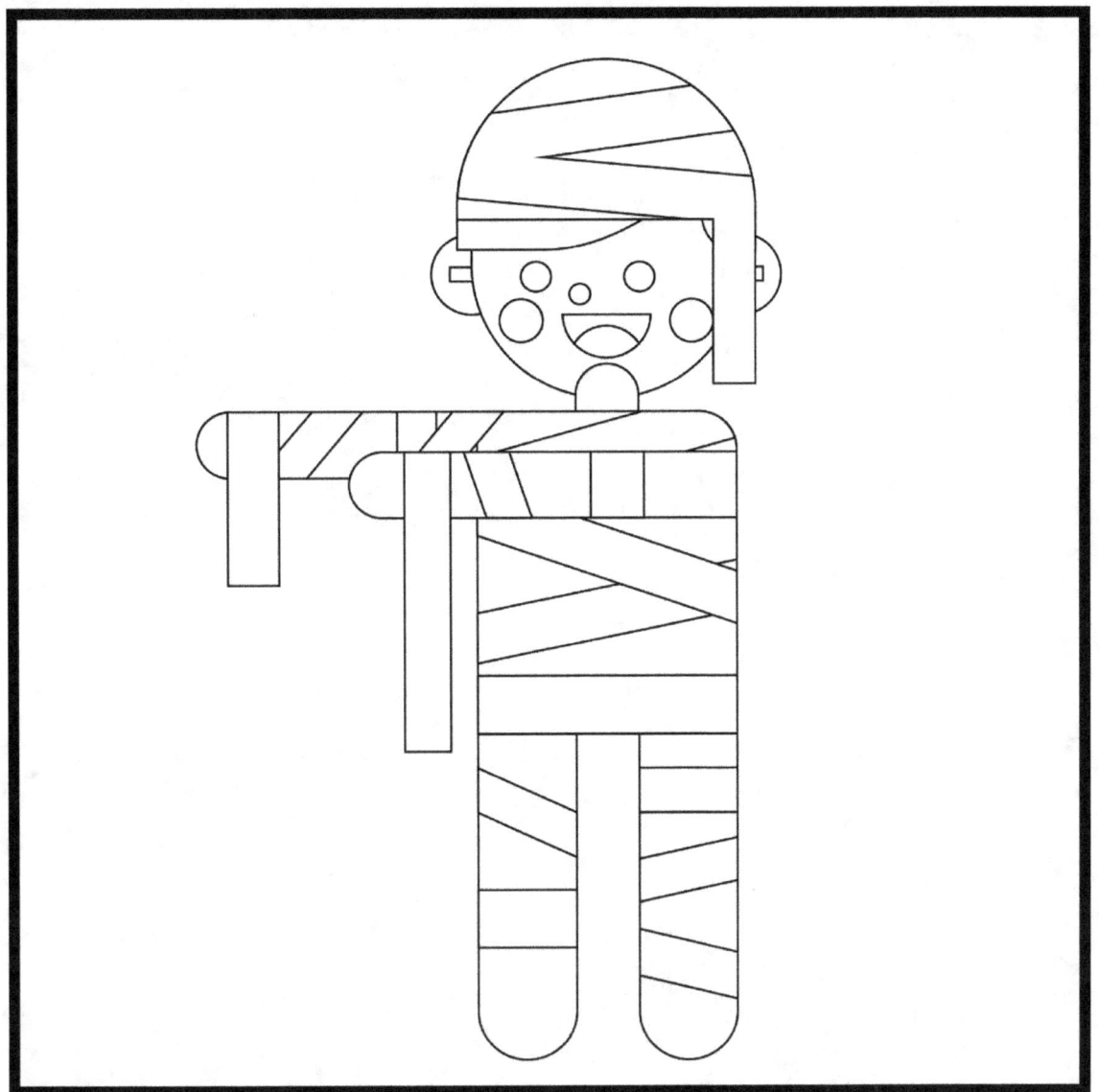

note:

_____

_____

_____

NOVEMBER 5TH

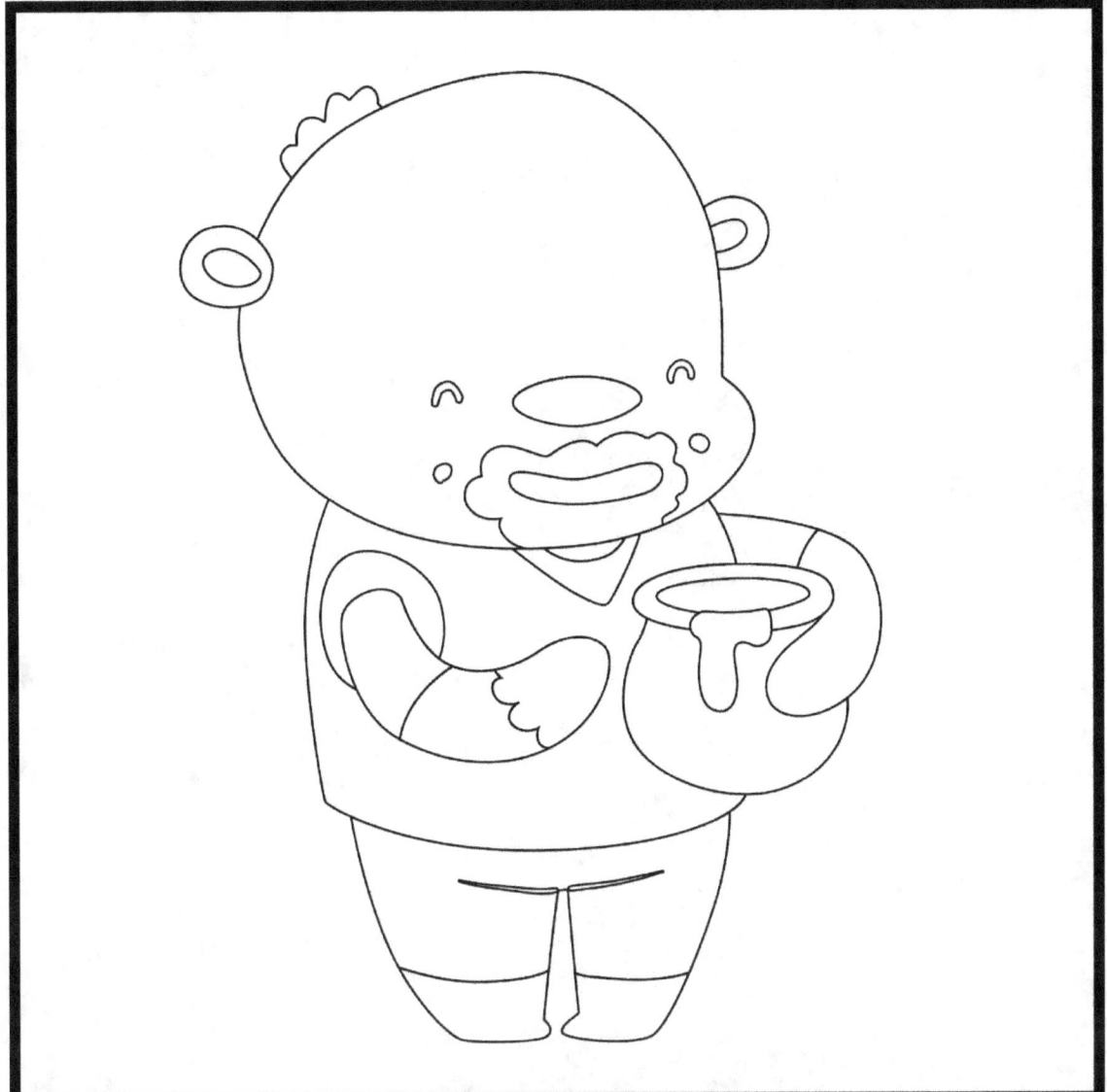

note:

_____

_____

_____

NOVEMBER 6TH

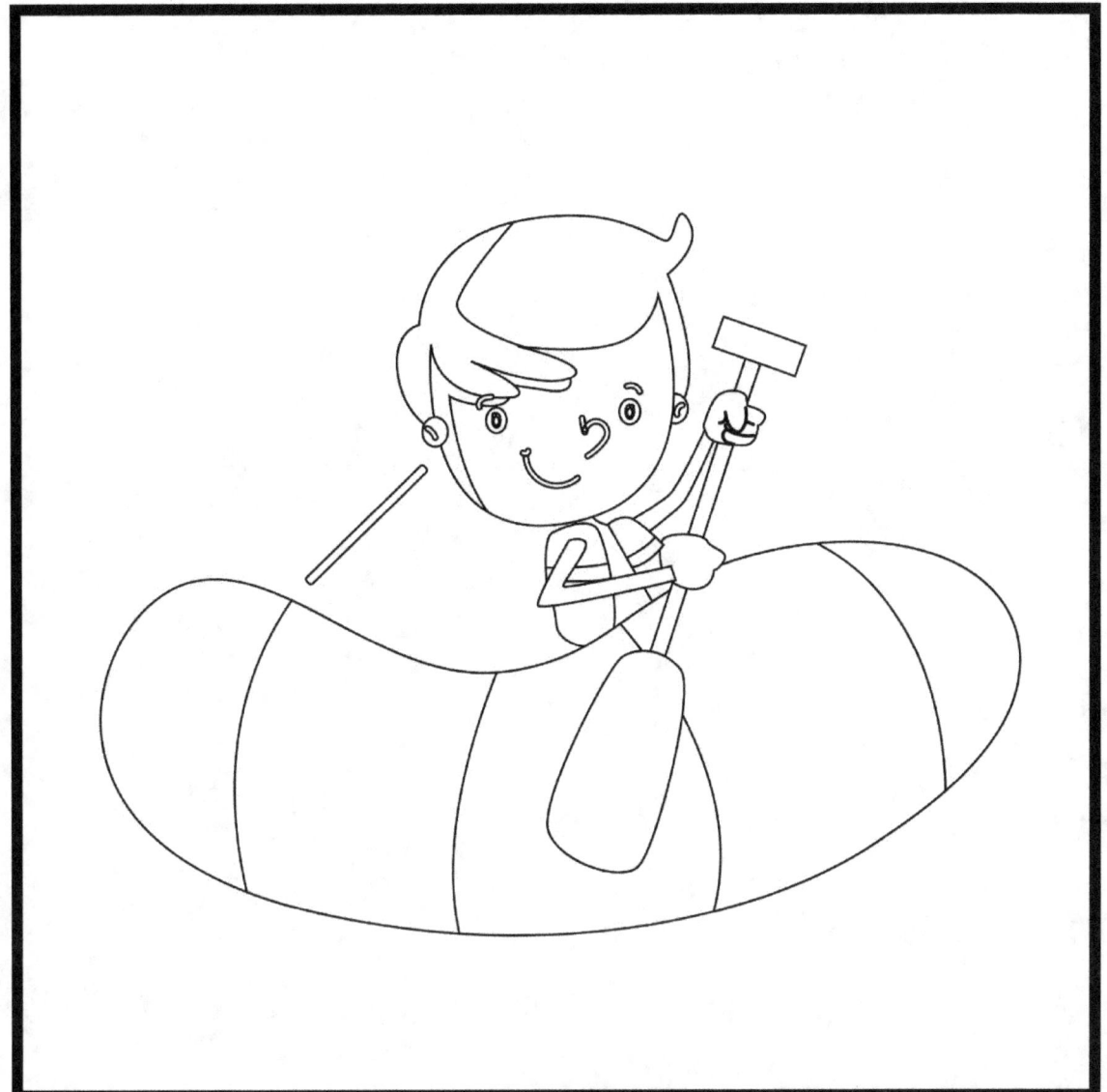

note:

_____

_____

_____

NOVEMBER 7TH

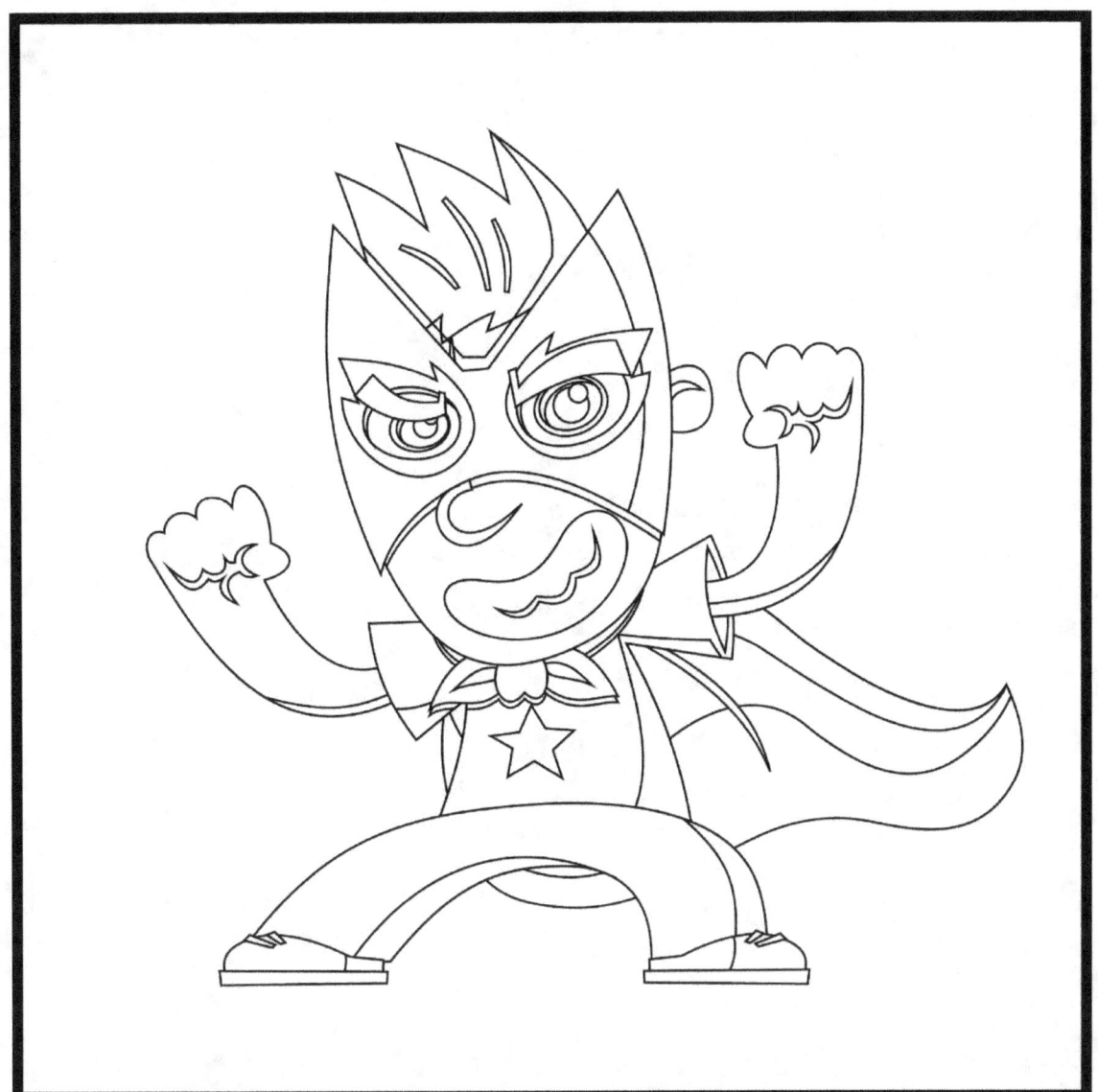

note:

_____

_____

_____

NOVEMBER 8TH

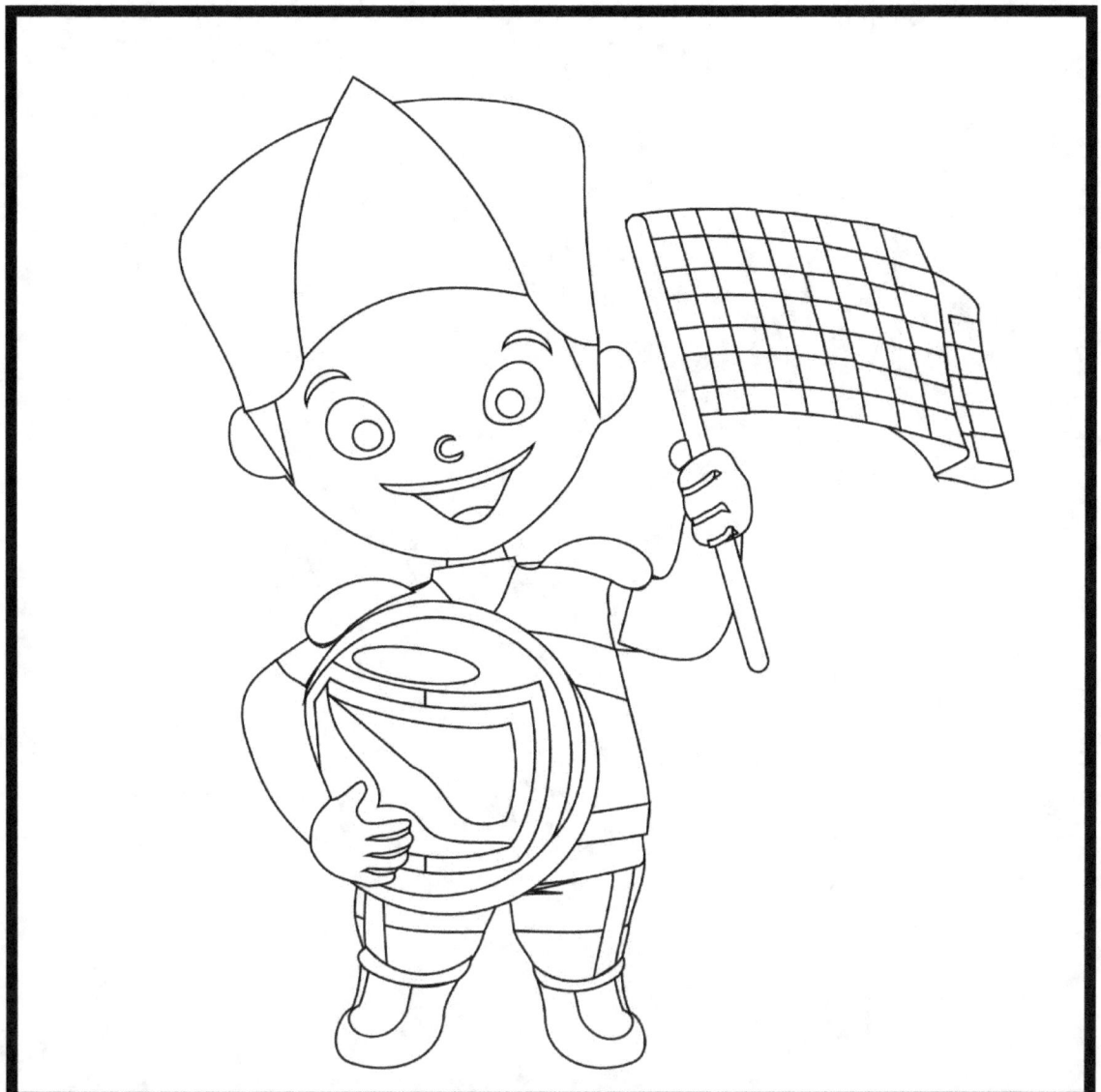

note:

_____

_____

_____

NOVEMBER 9TH

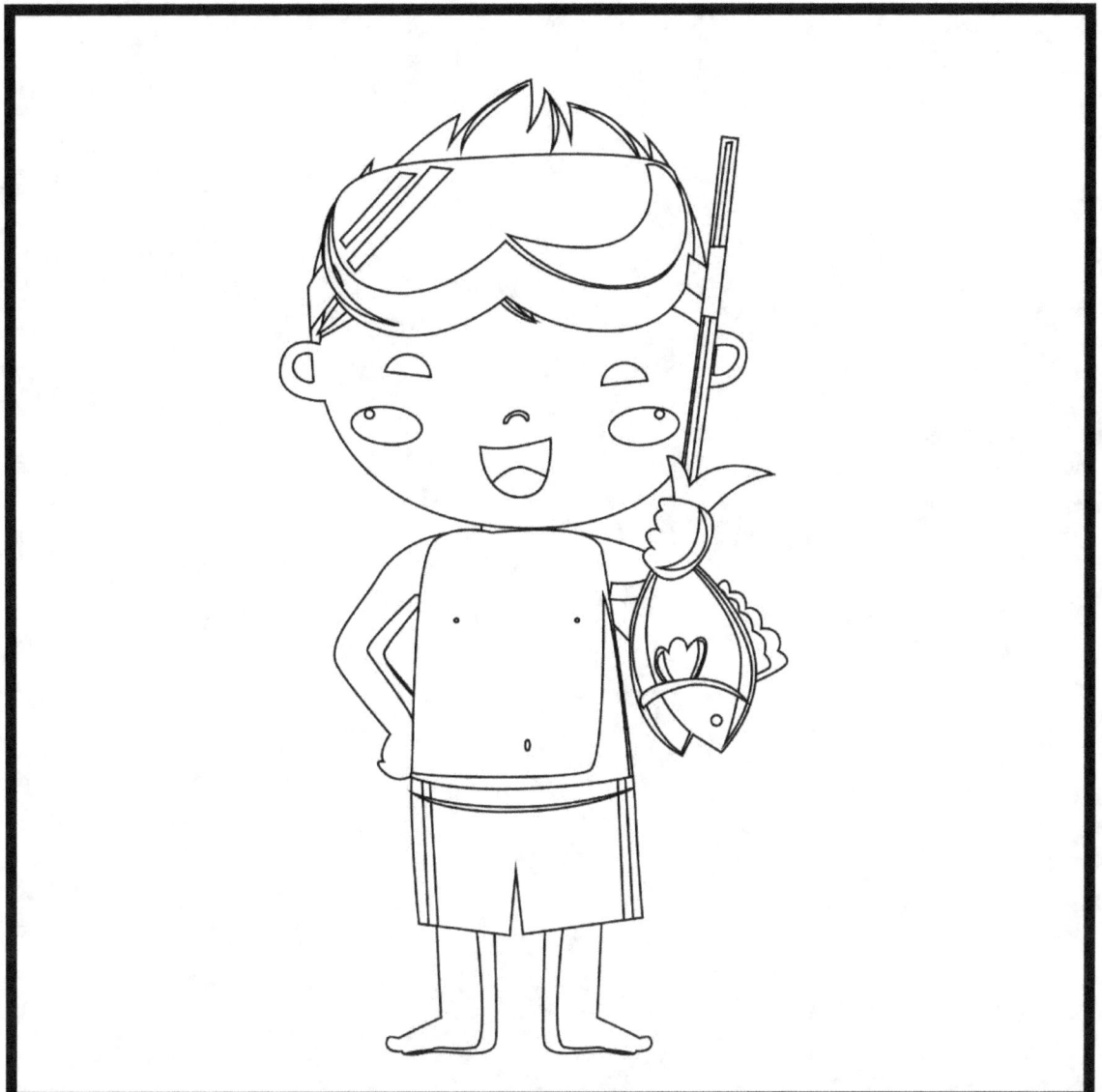

note:

_____

_____

_____

NOVEMBER 10TH

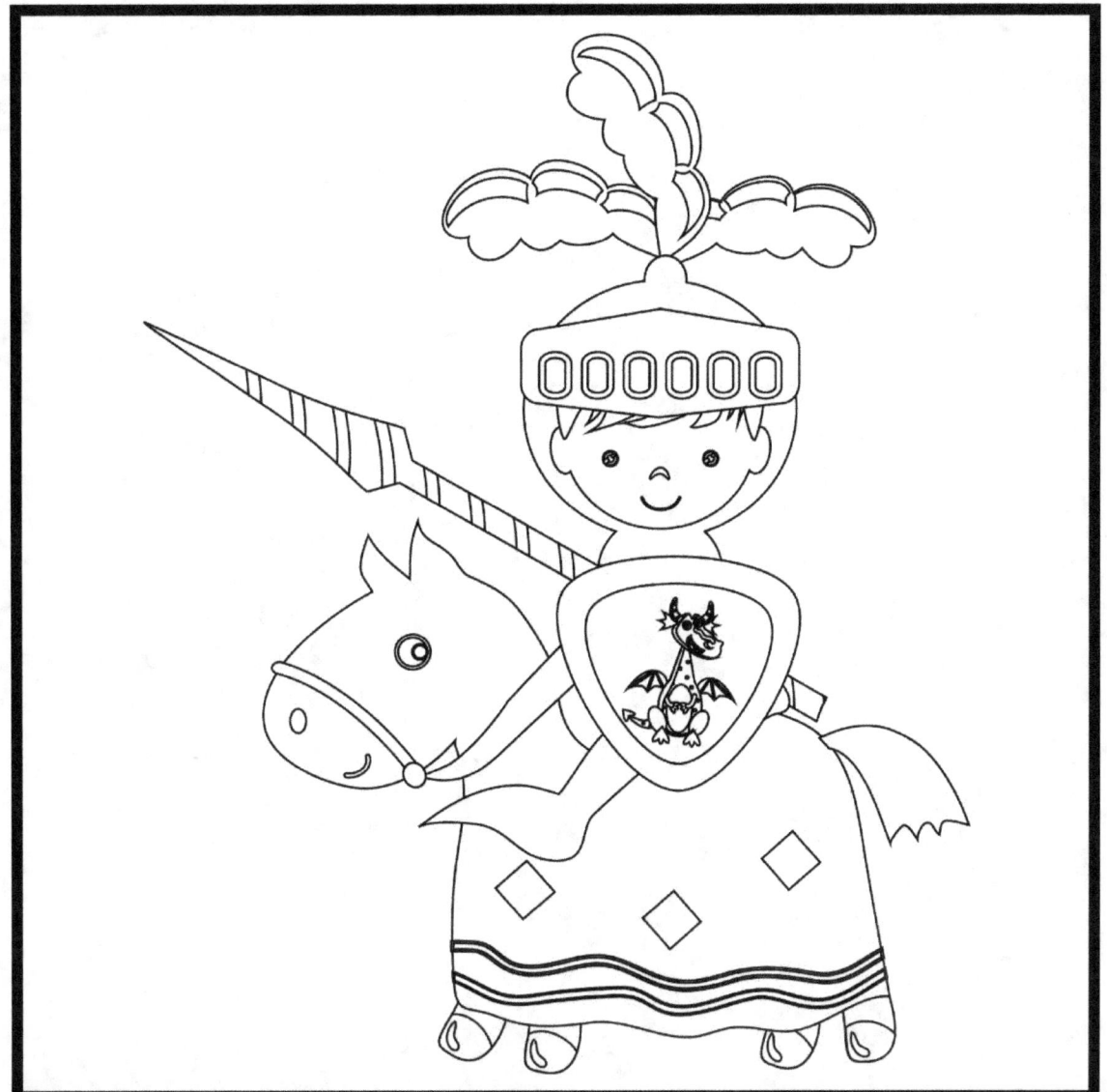

note:

_____

_____

_____

NOVEMBER 11TH

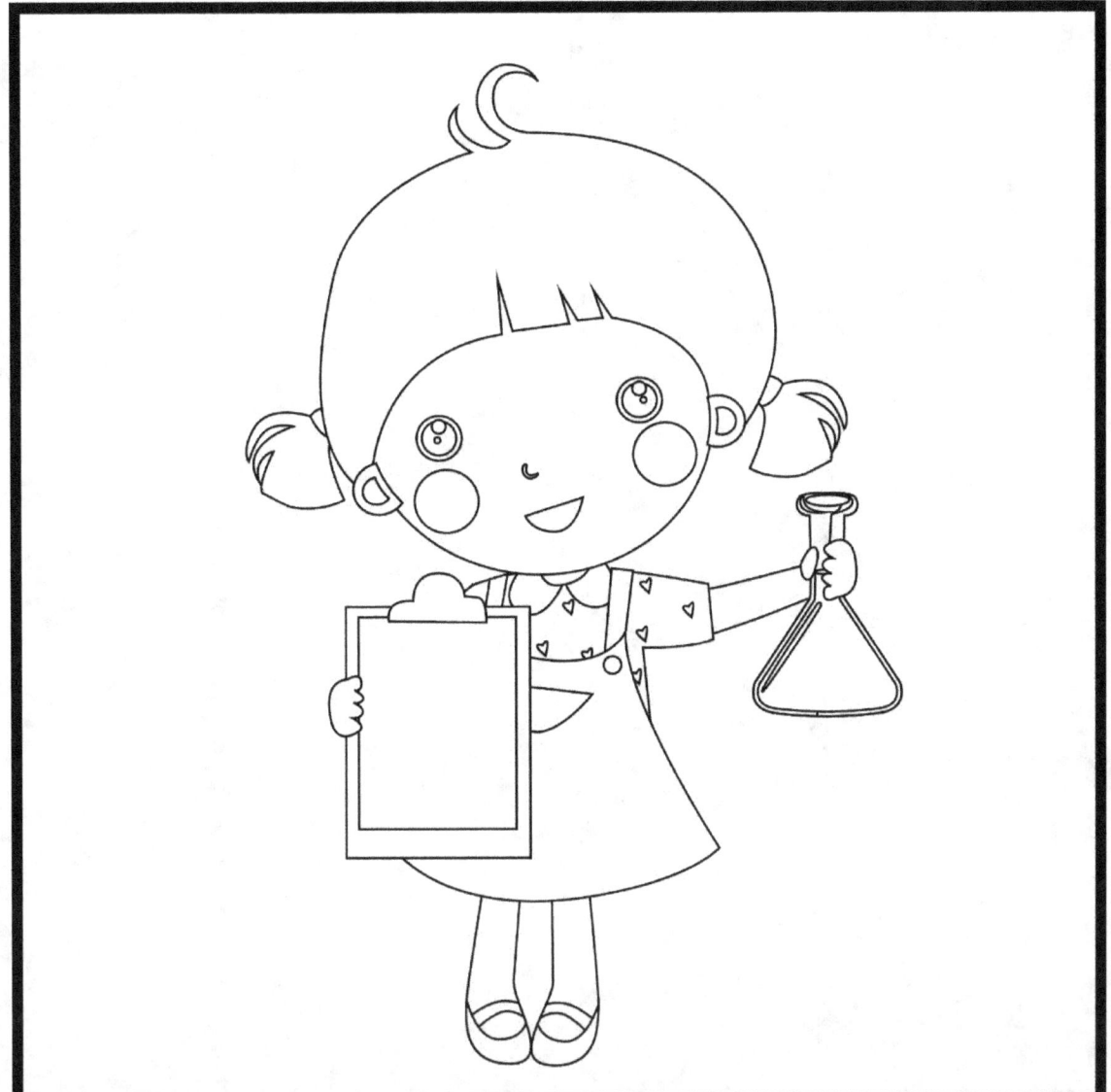

note:

_____

_____

_____

NOVEMBER 12TH

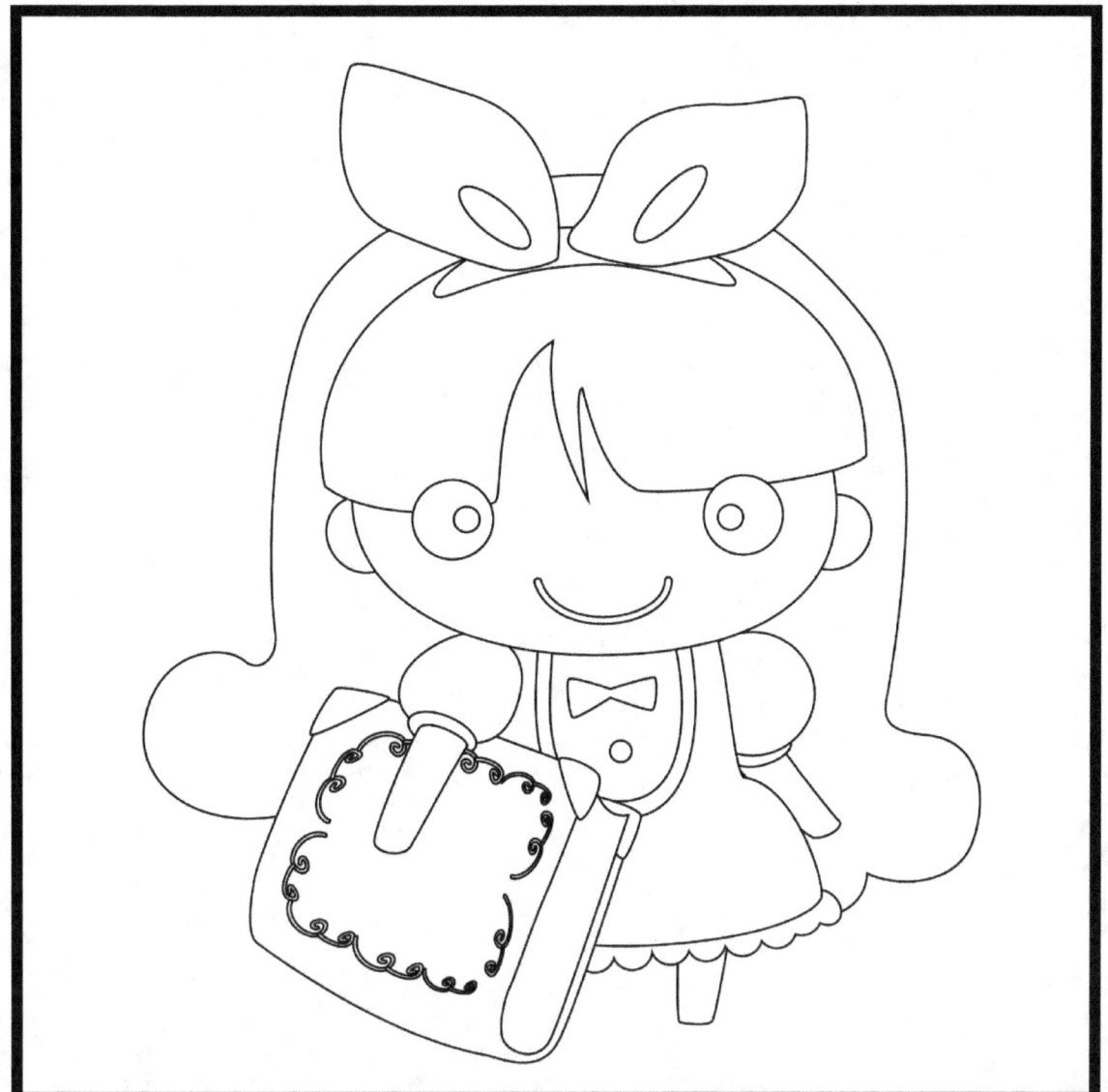

note:

_____

_____

_____

NOVEMBER 13TH

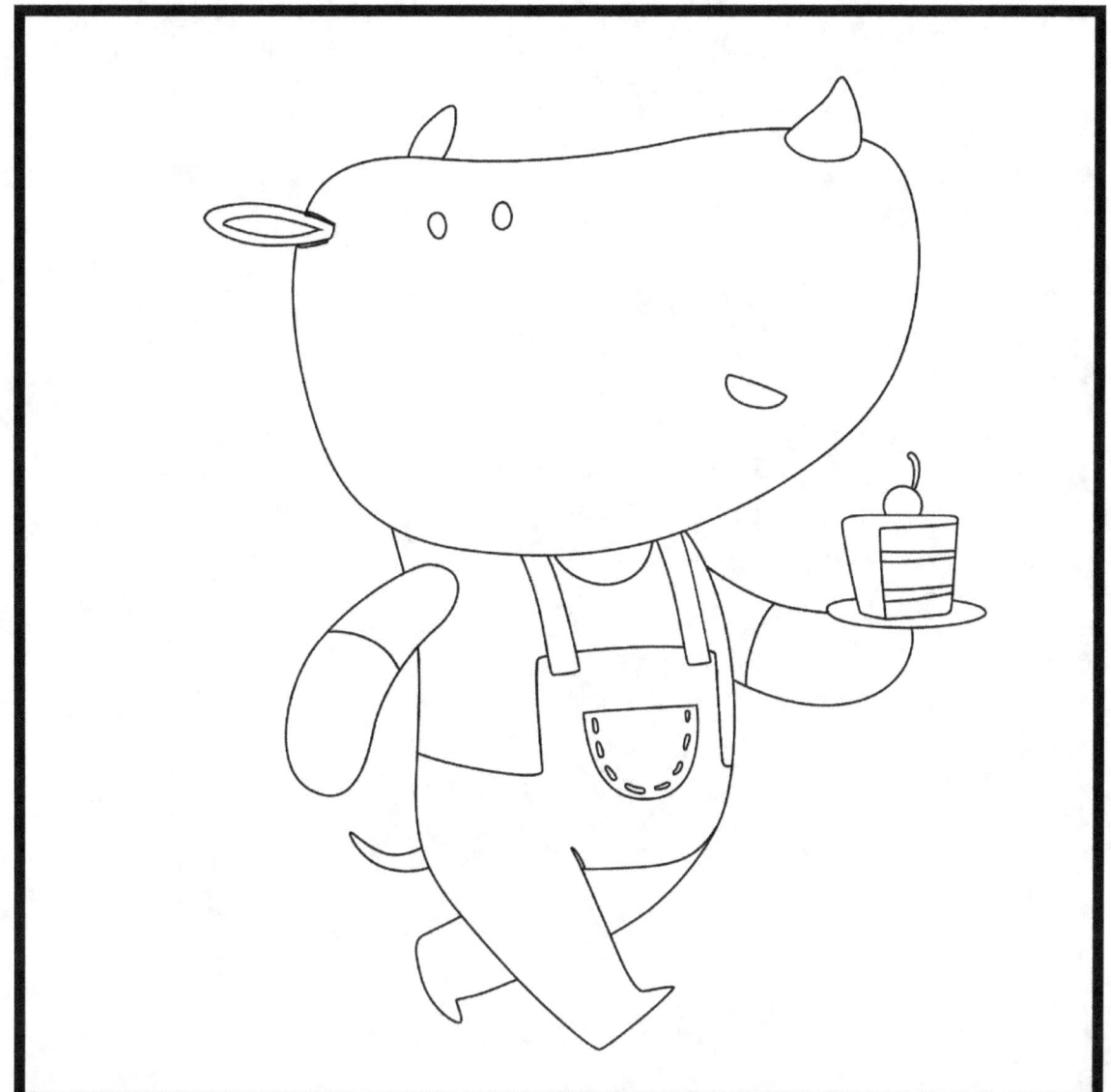

note:

_____

_____

_____

NOVEMBER 14TH

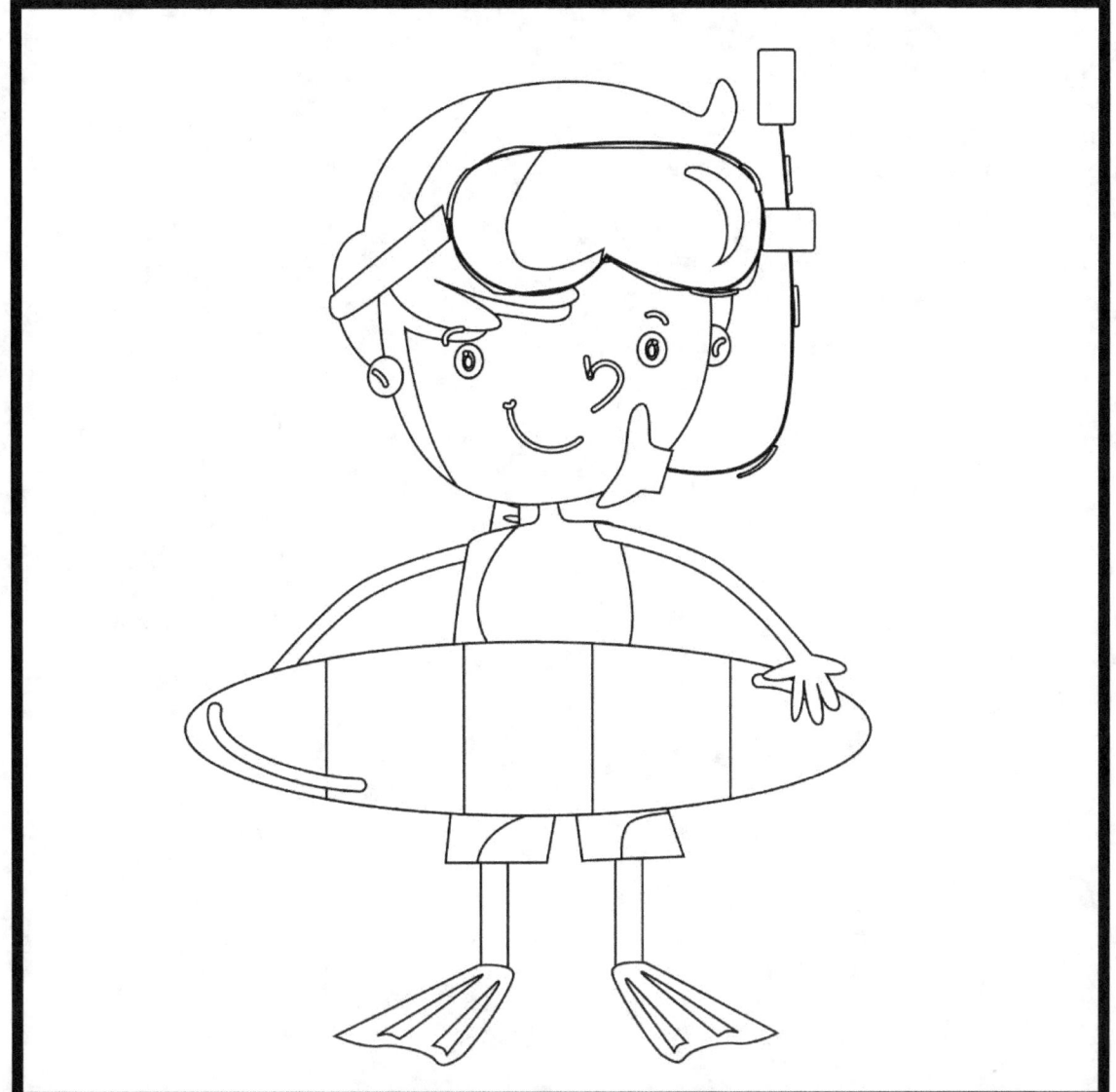

note:

_____

_____

_____

NOVEMBER 15TH

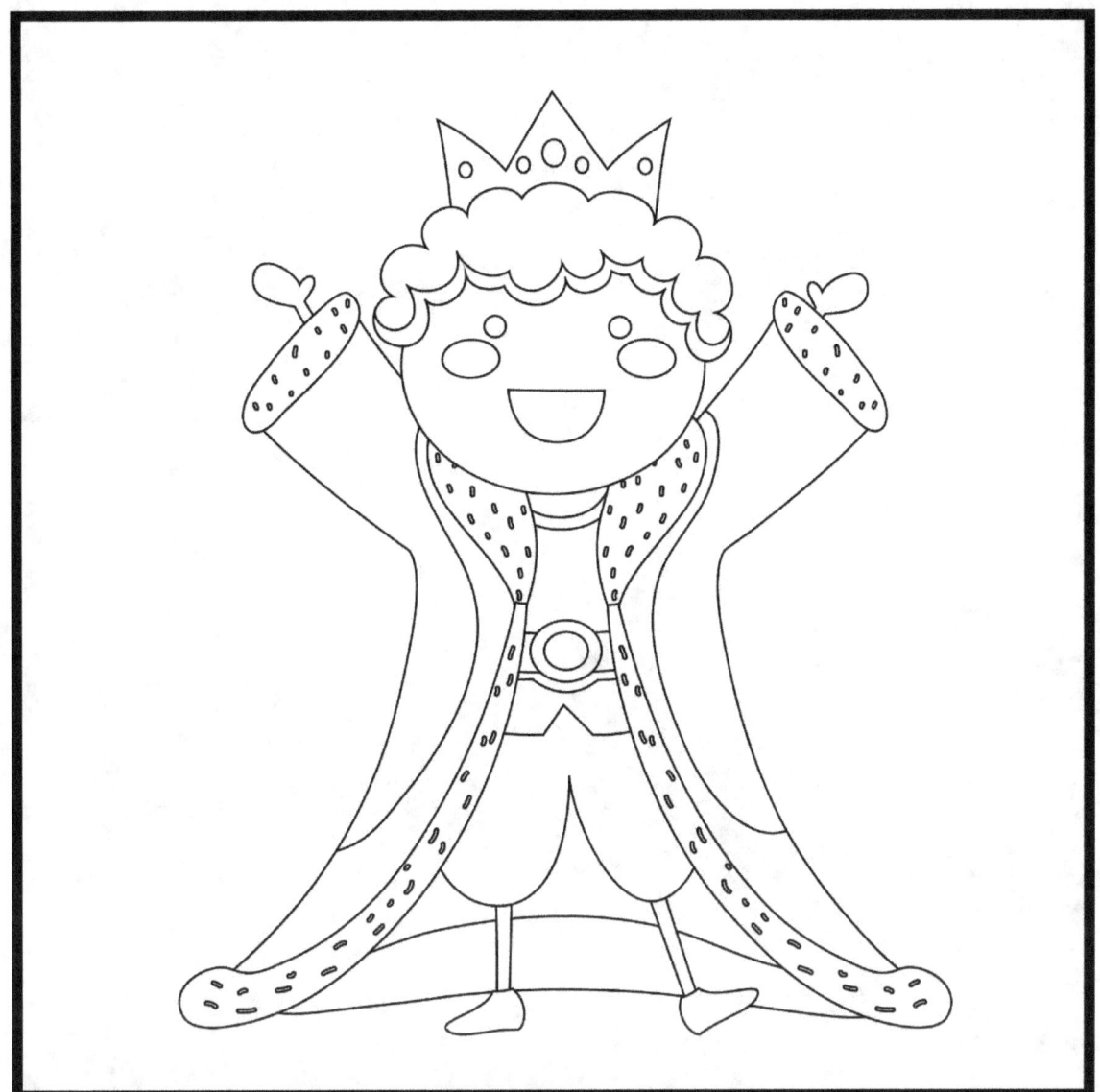

note:

_____

_____

_____

NOVEMBER 16TH

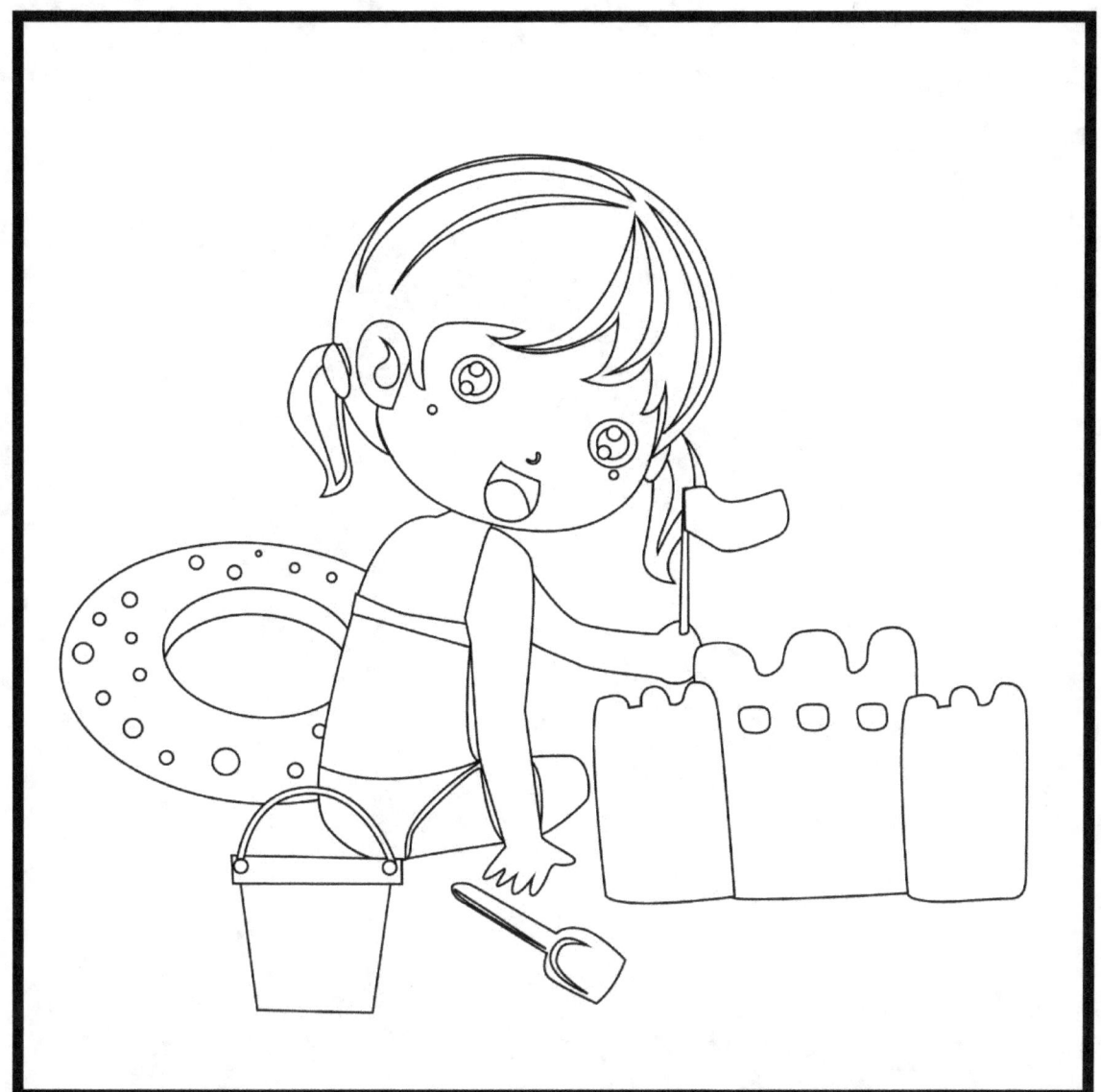

note:

_____

_____

_____

NOVEMBER 17TH

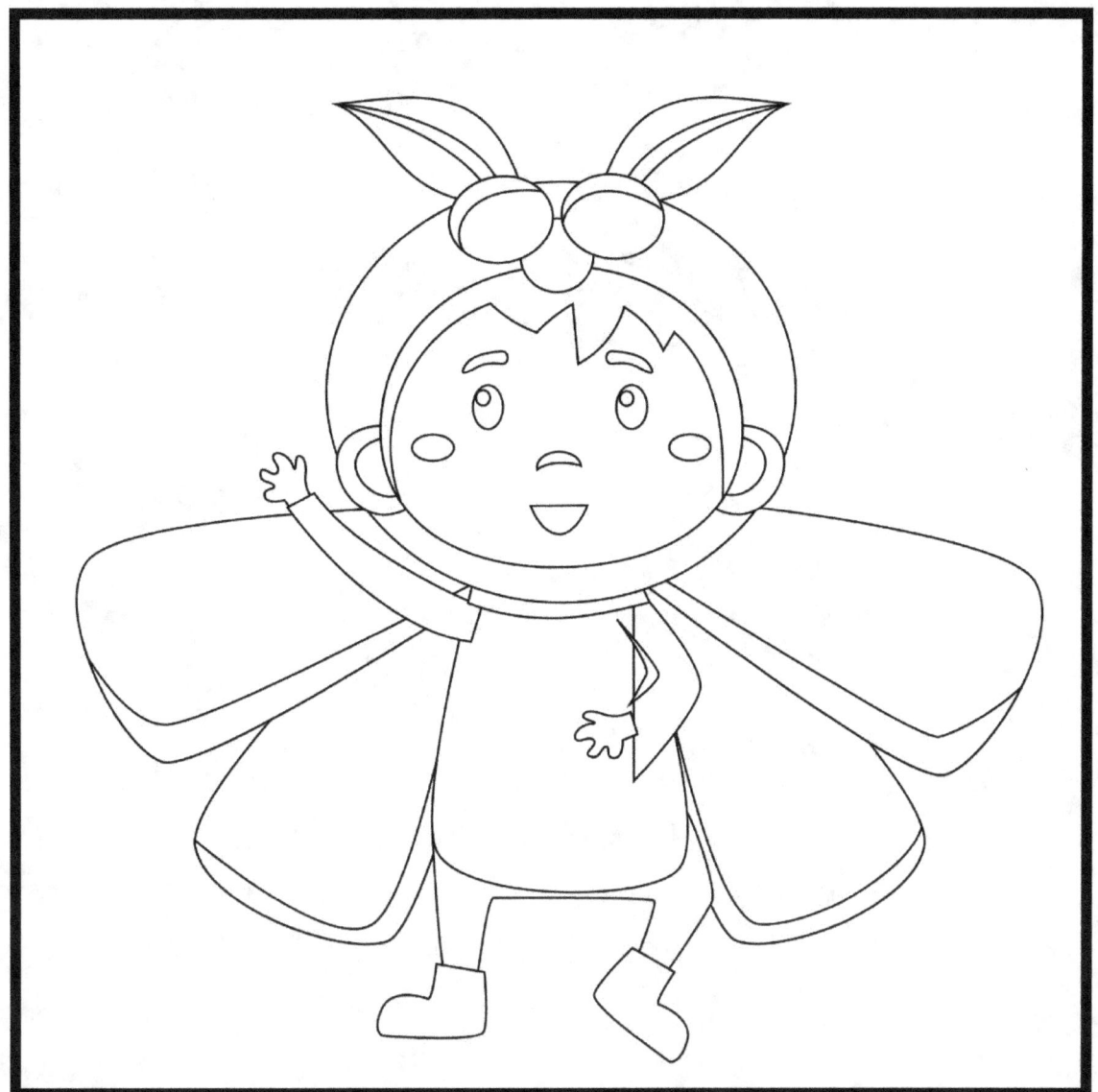

note:

_____

_____

_____

NOVEMBER 18TH

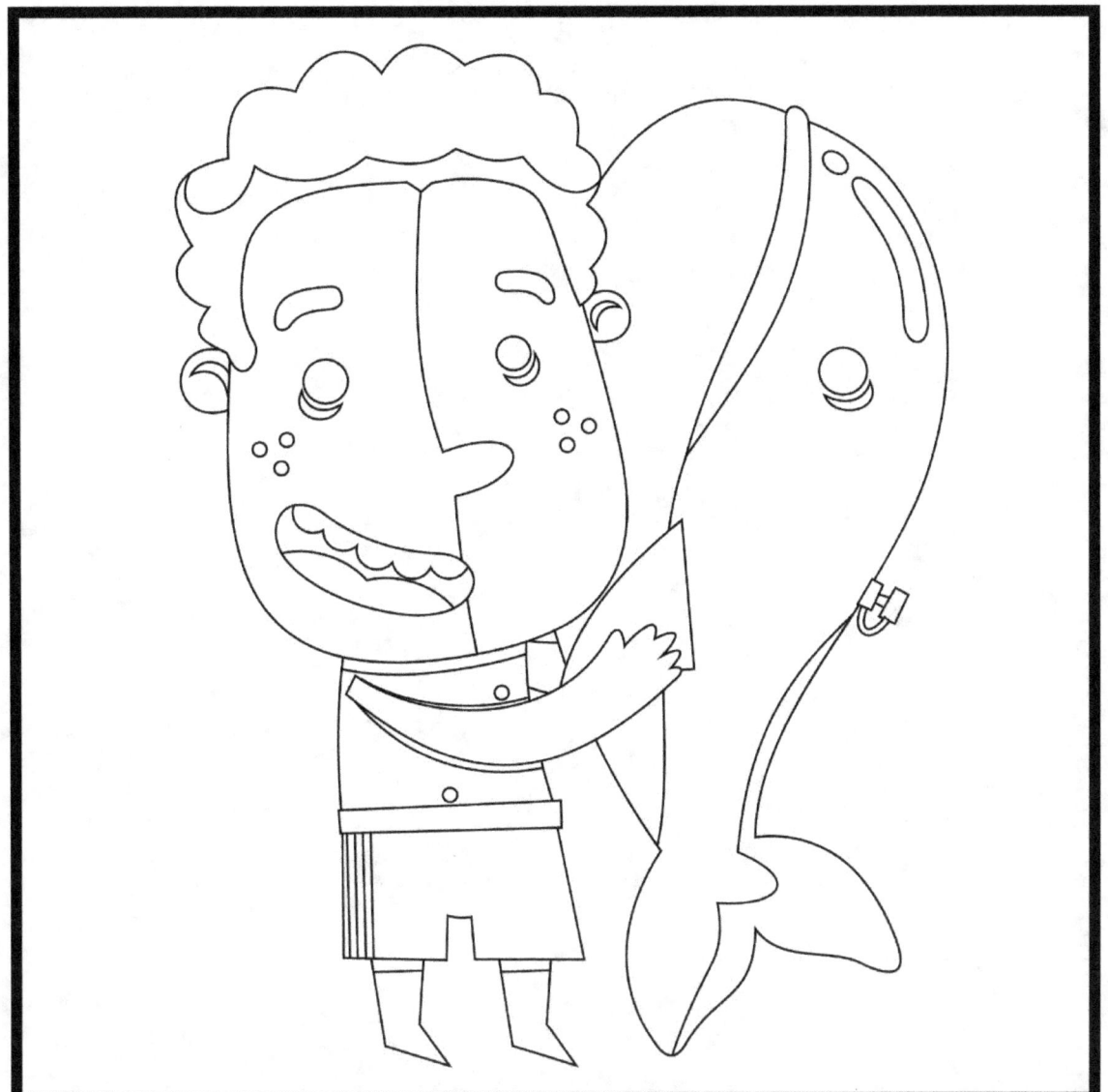

note:

_____

_____

_____

NOVEMBER 19TH

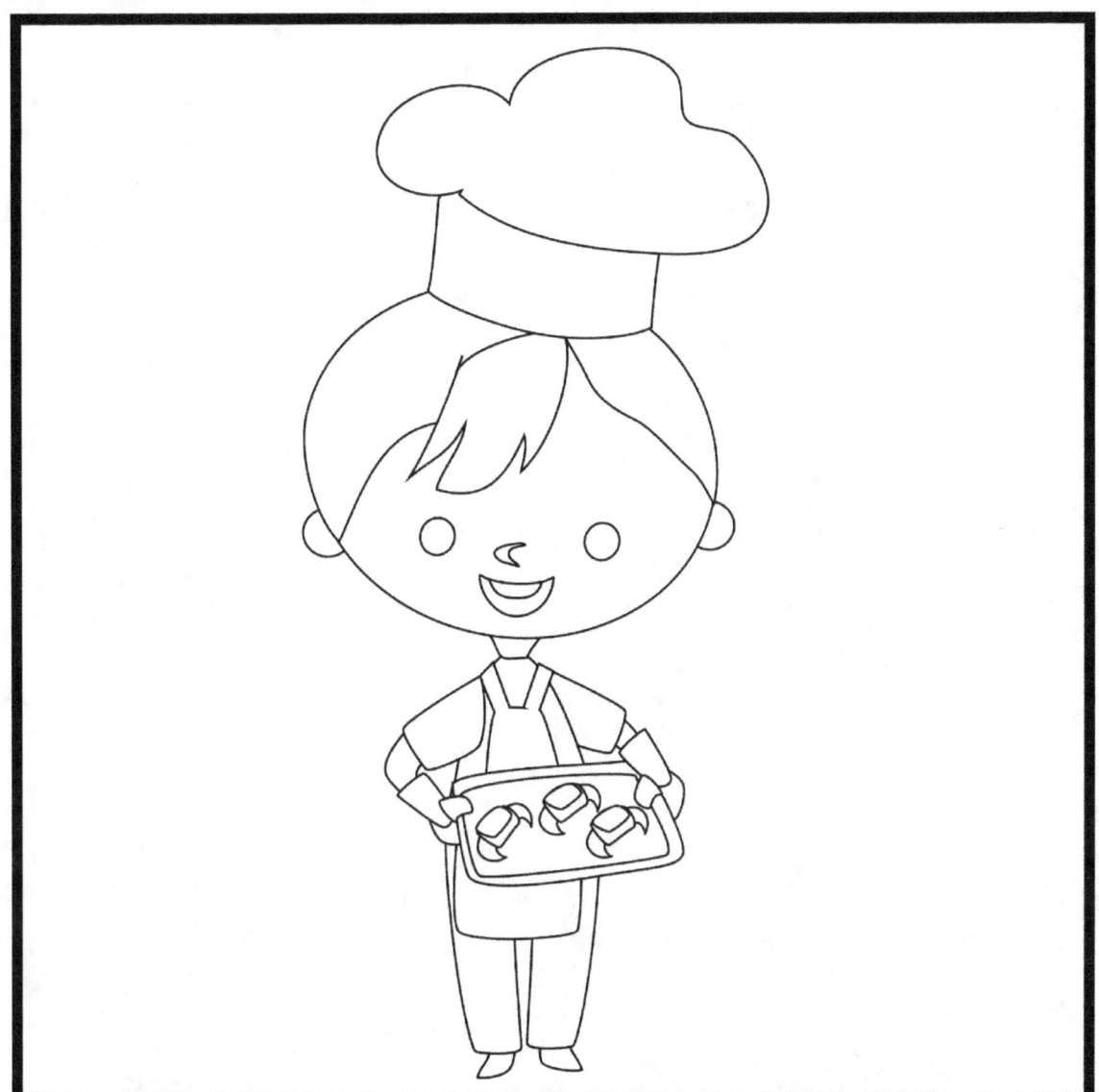

note:

_____

_____

_____

NOVEMBER 20TH

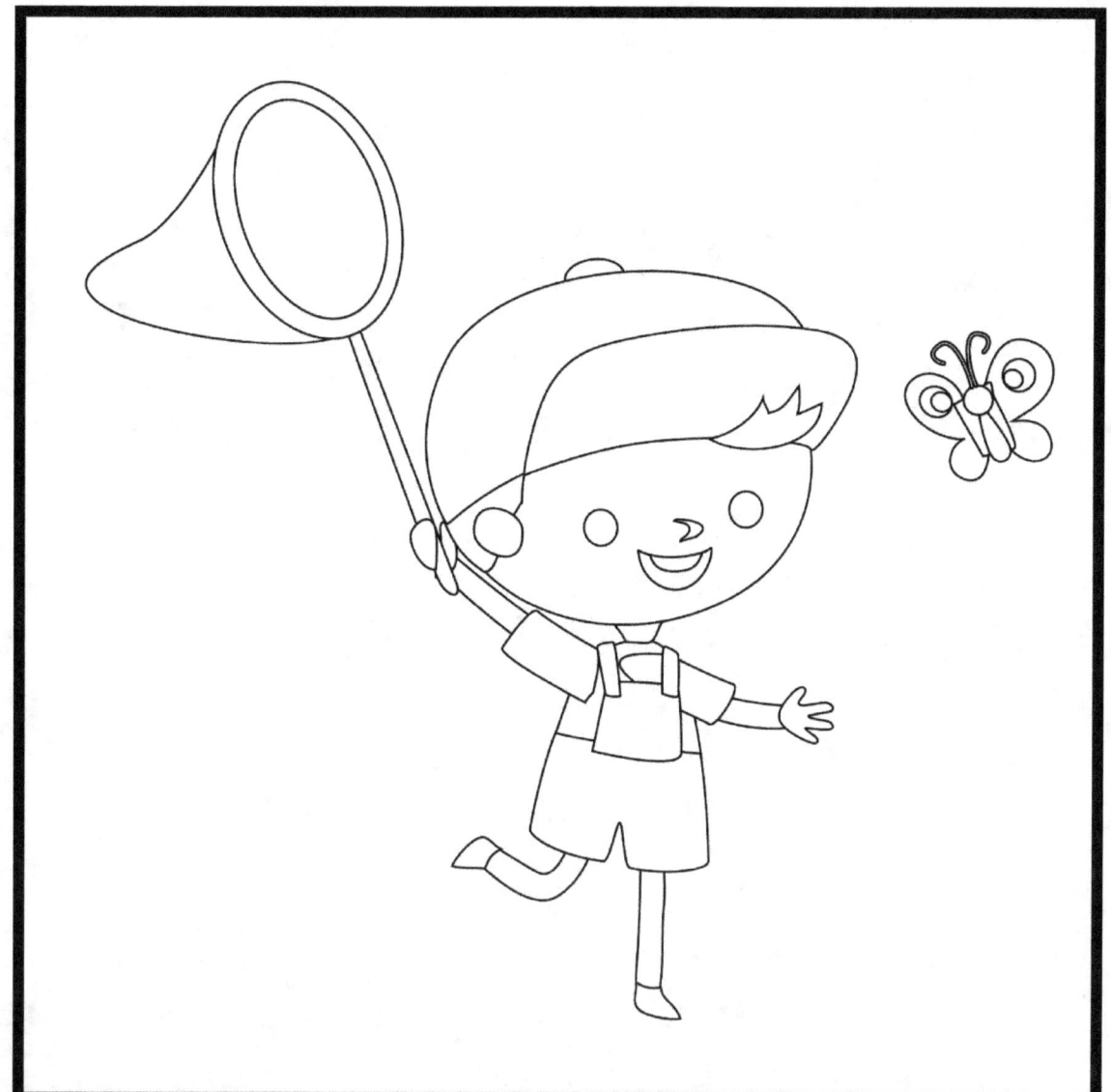

note:

_____

_____

_____

NOVEMBER 21TH

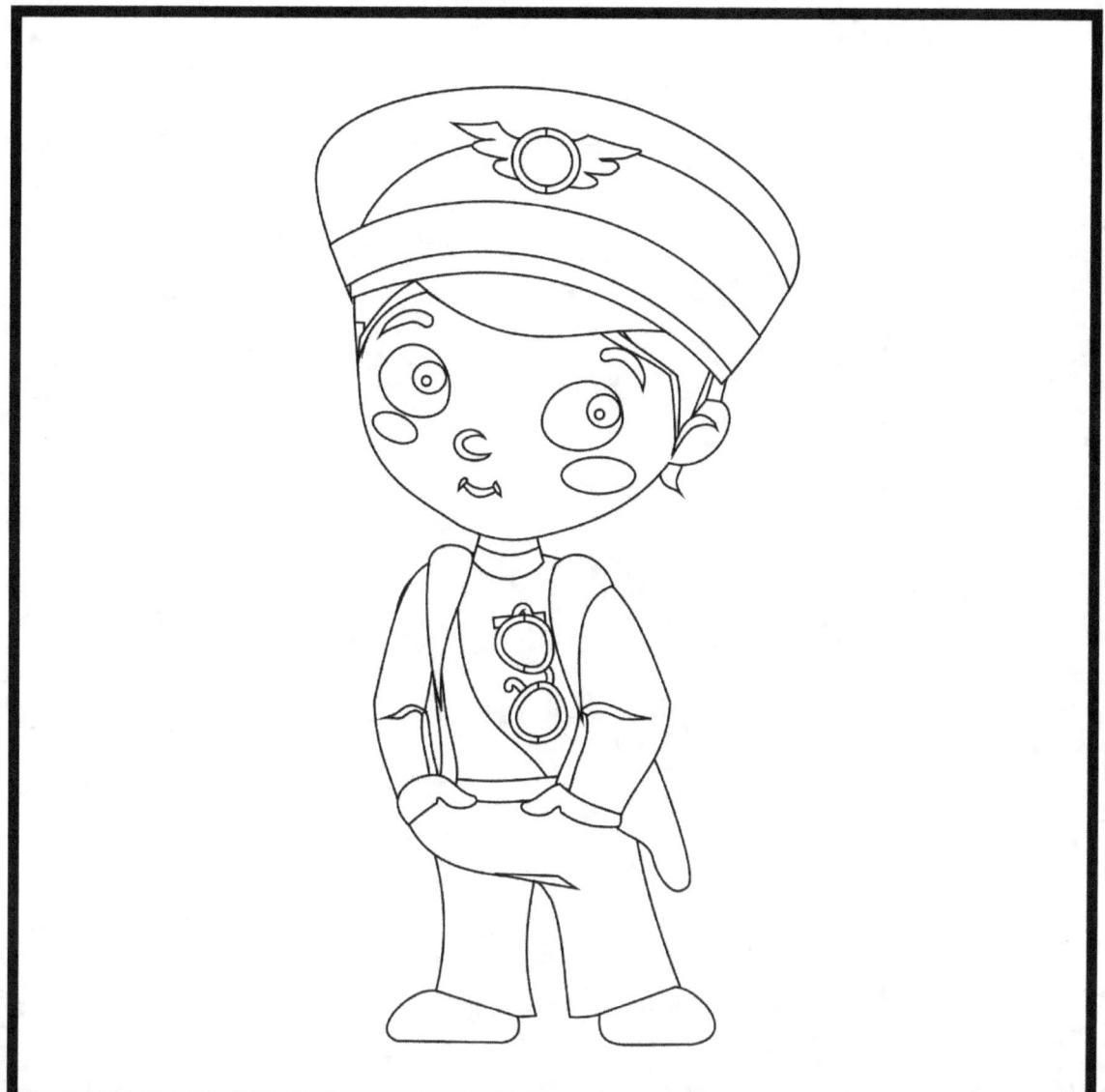

note:

_____

_____

_____

NOVEMBER 22TH

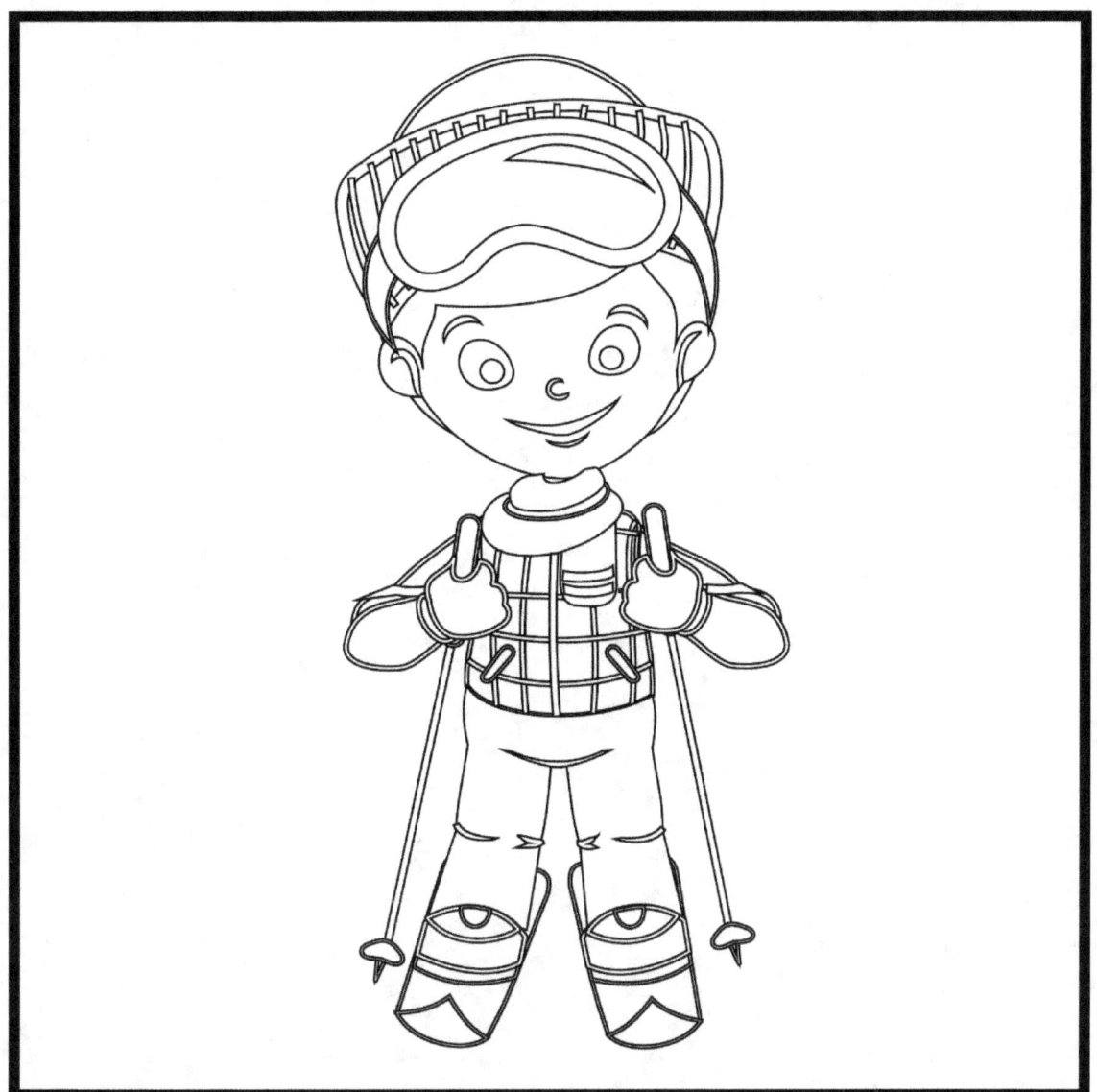

note:

_____

_____

_____

NOVEMBER 23TH

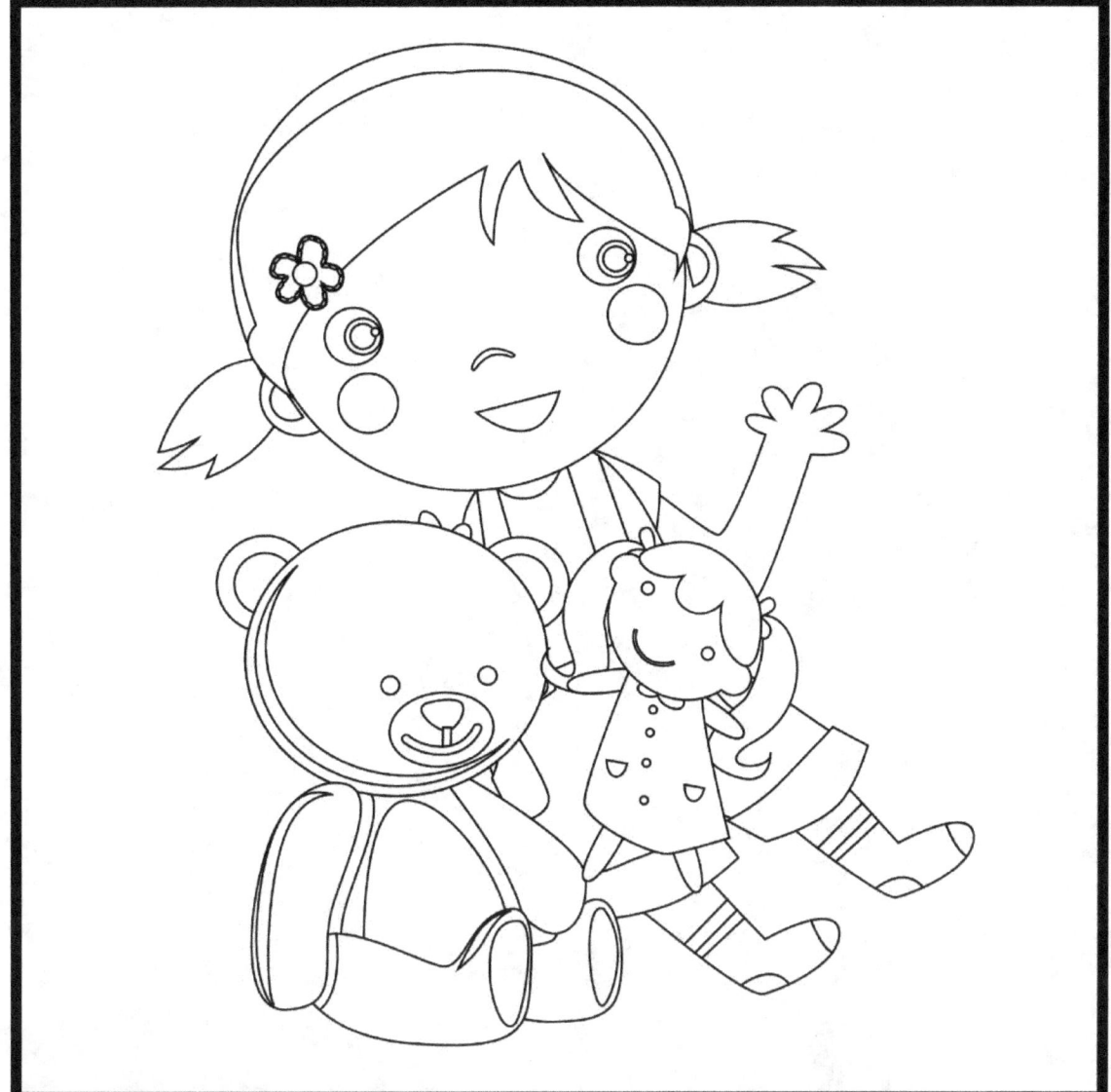

note:

_____

_____

_____

NOVEMBER 24TH

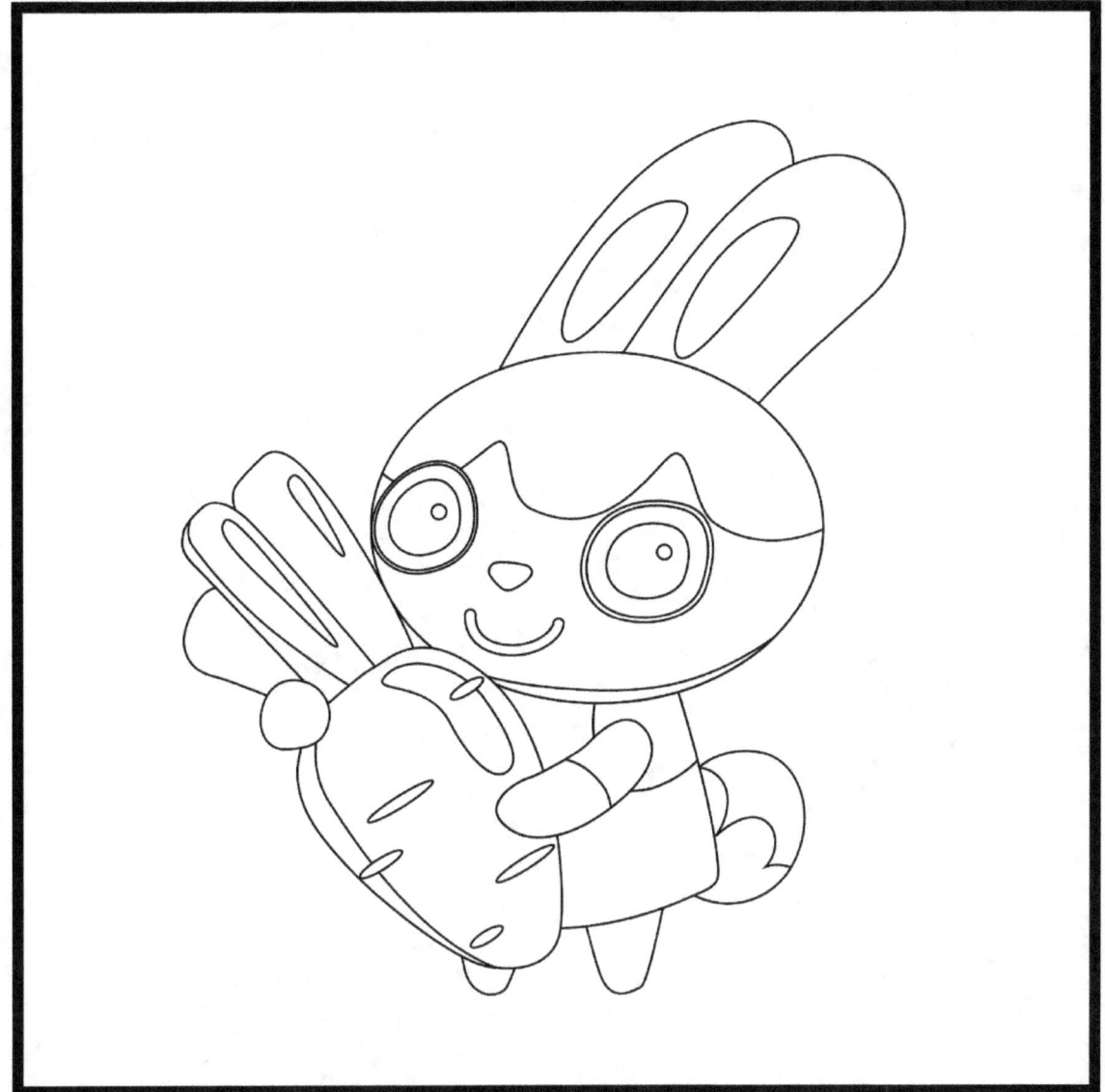

note:

_____

_____

_____

NOVEMBER 25TH

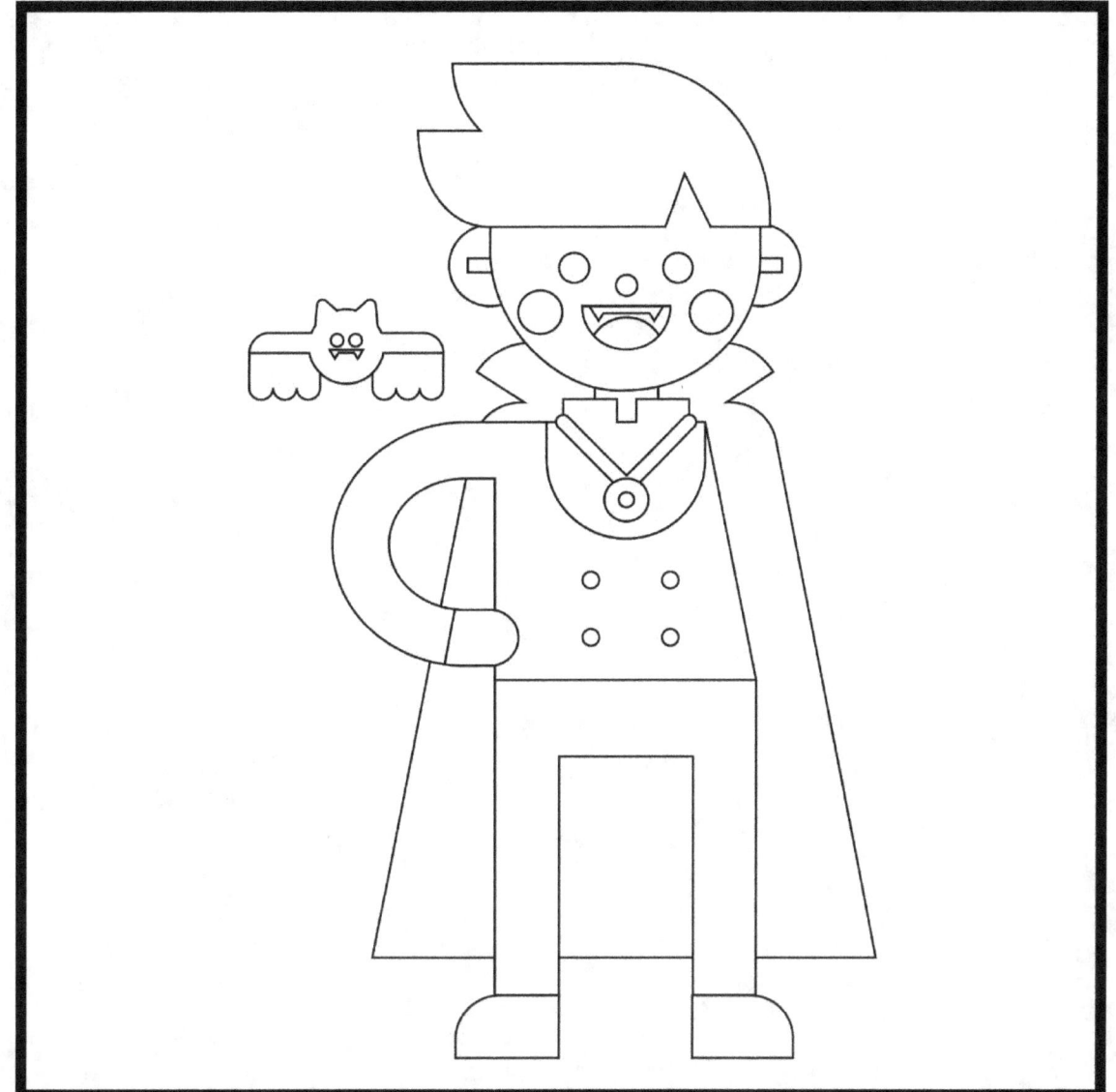

note:

_____

_____

_____

NOVEMBER 26TH

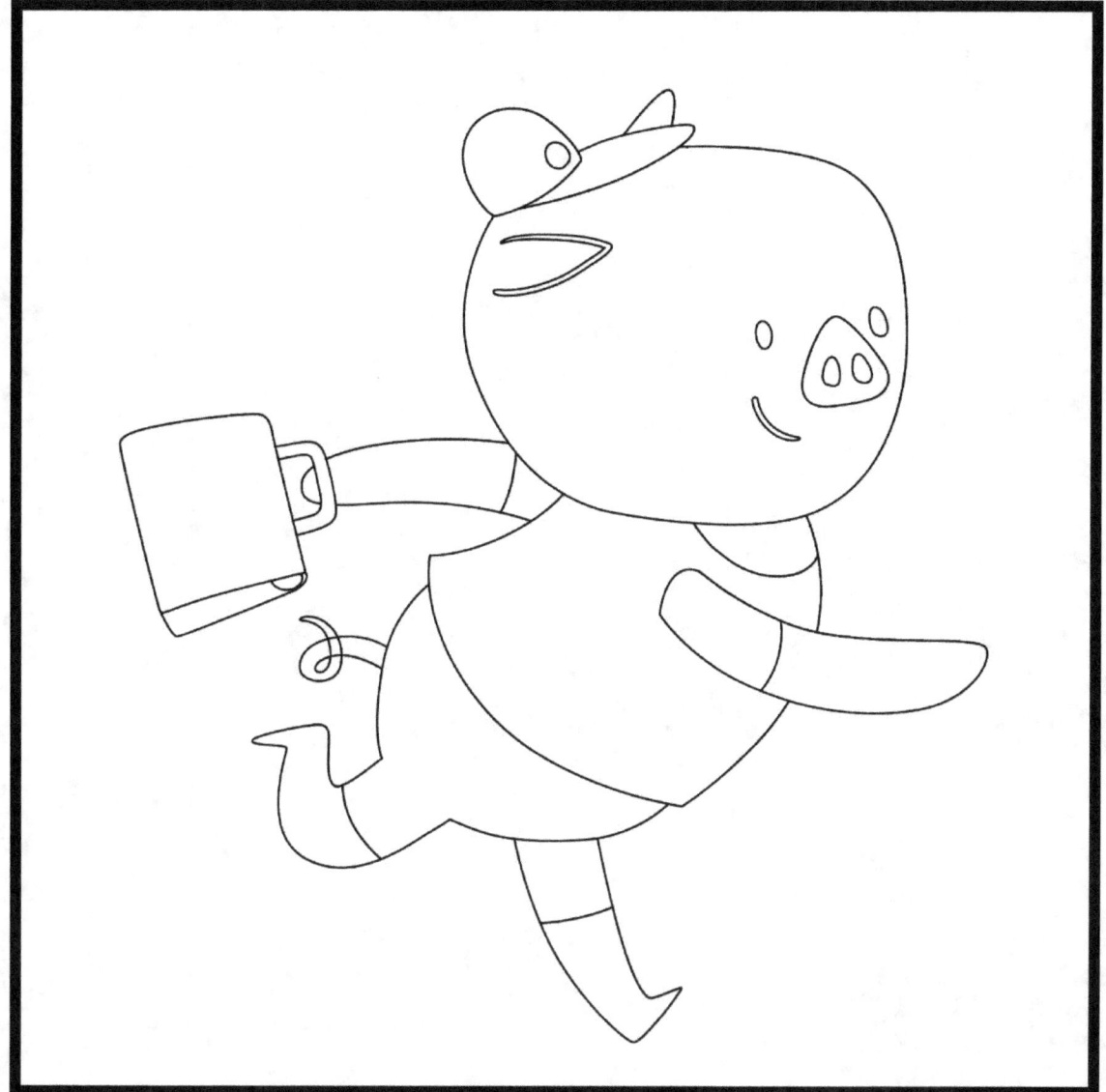

note:

_____

_____

_____

NOVEMBER 27TH

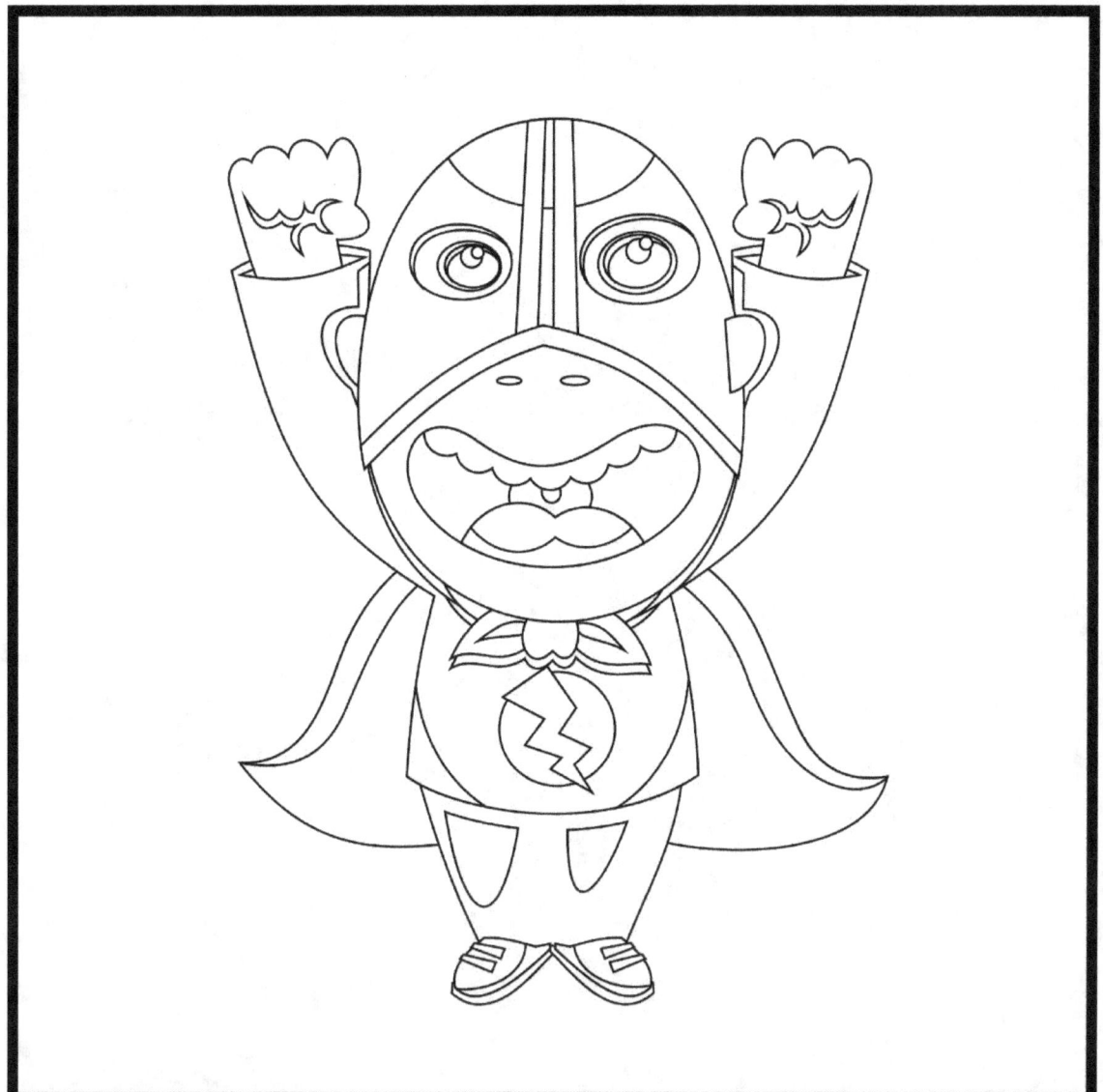

note:

_____

_____

_____

NOVEMBER 28TH

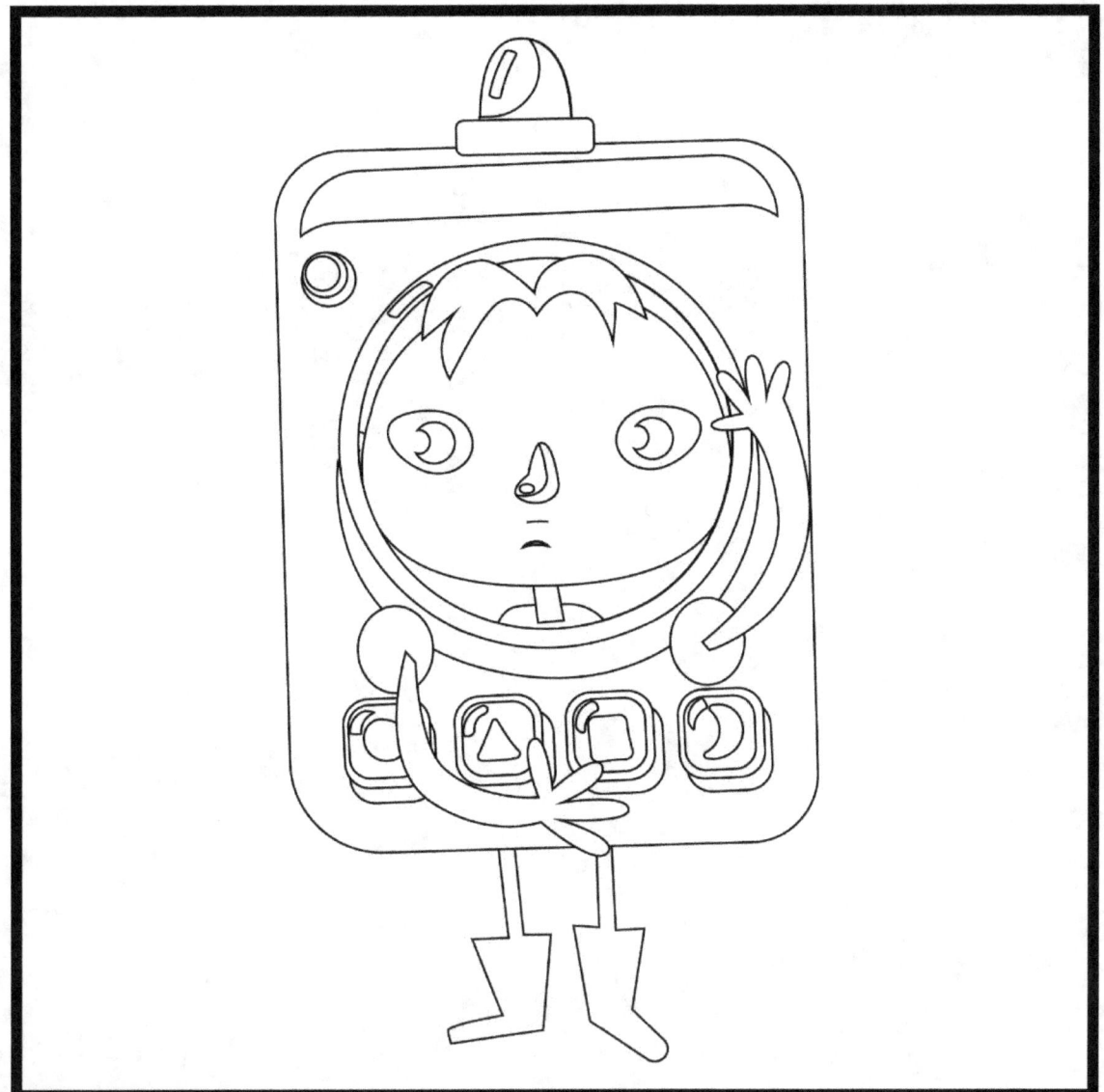

note:

_____

_____

_____

NOVEMBER 29TH

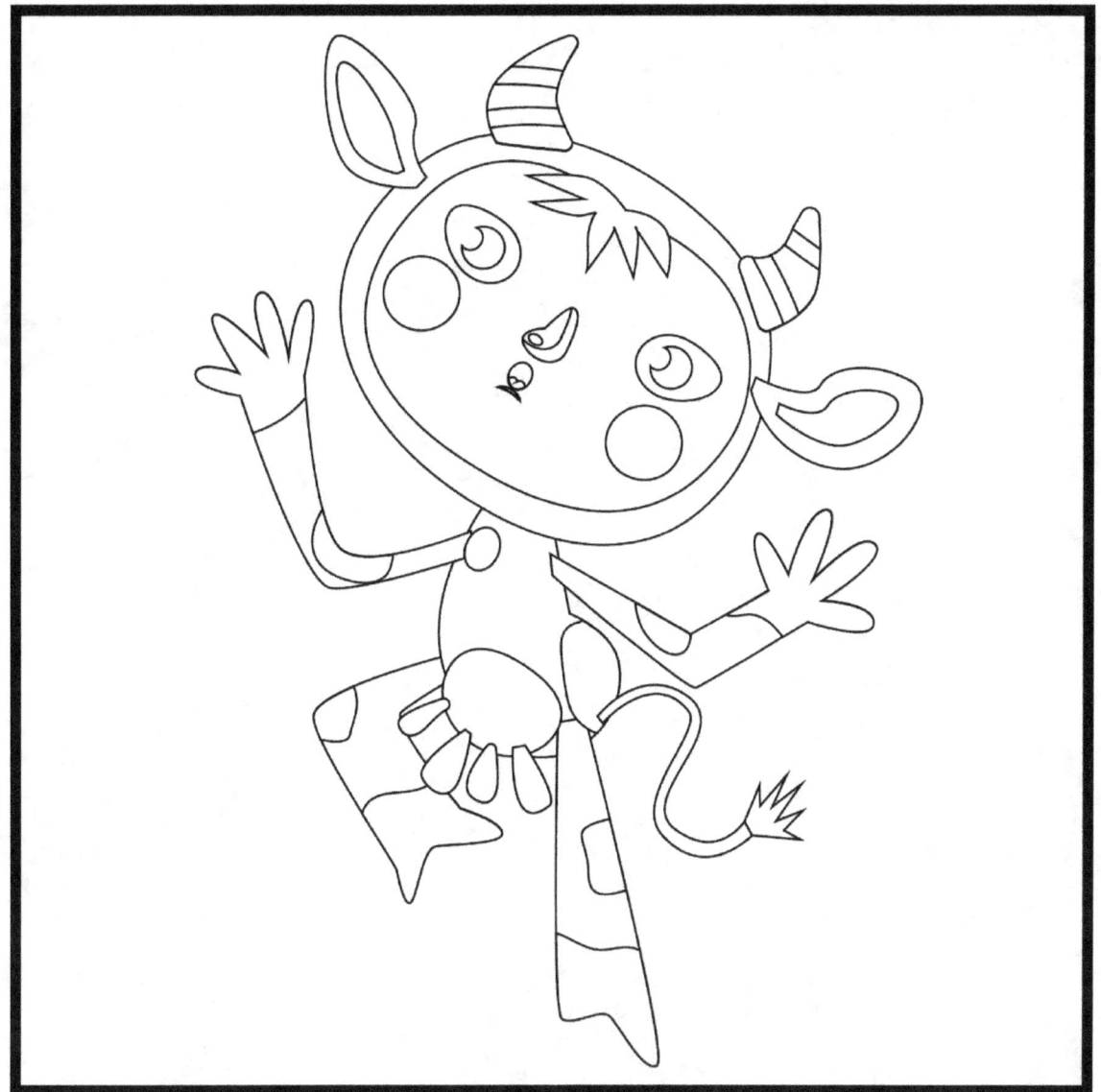

note:

_____

_____

_____

NOVEMBER 30TH

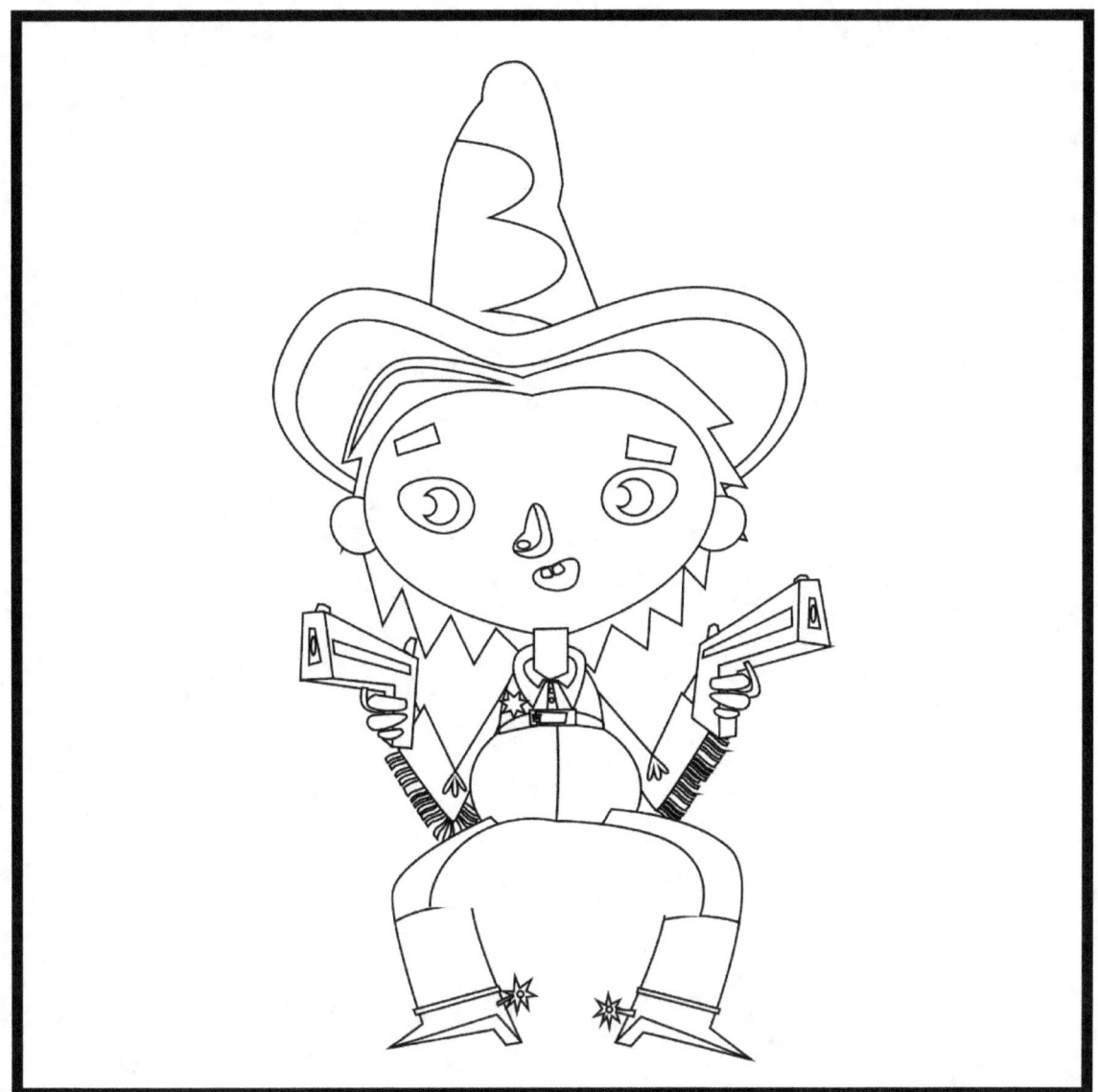

note:

_____

_____

_____

NOVEMBER 31TH

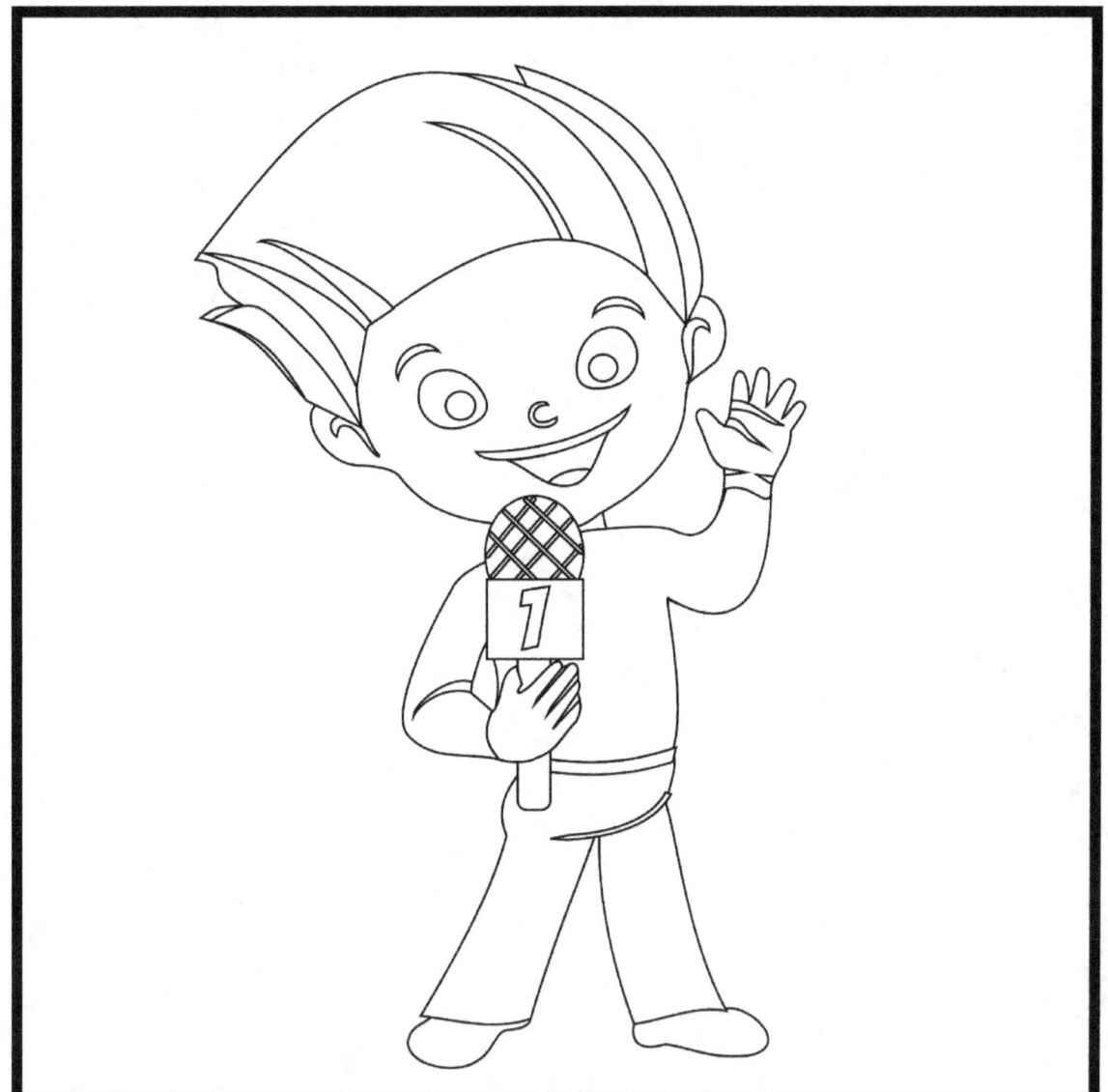

note:

_____

_____

_____

NOVEMBER 32TH

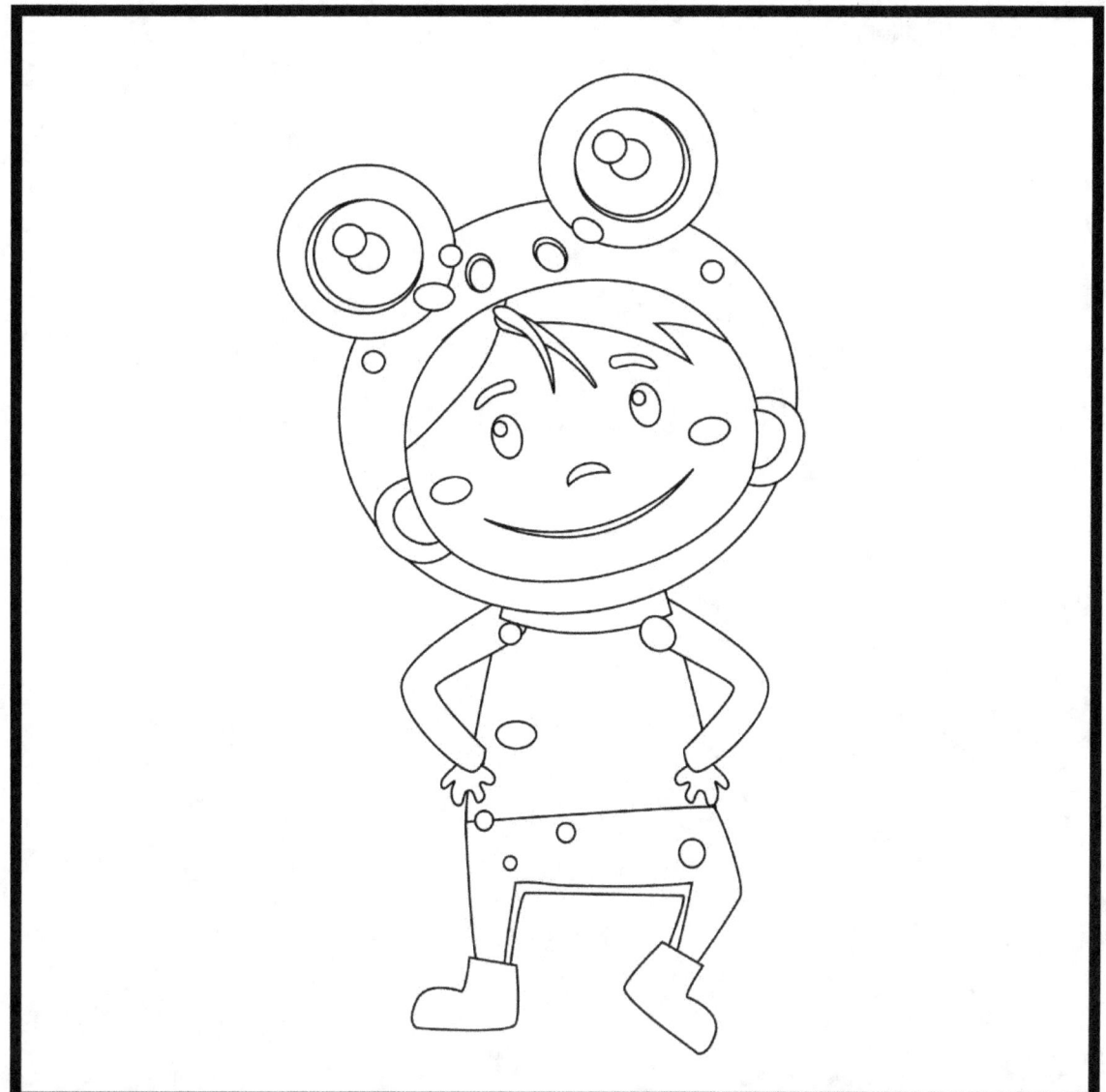

note:

_____

_____

_____

NOVEMBER 33TH

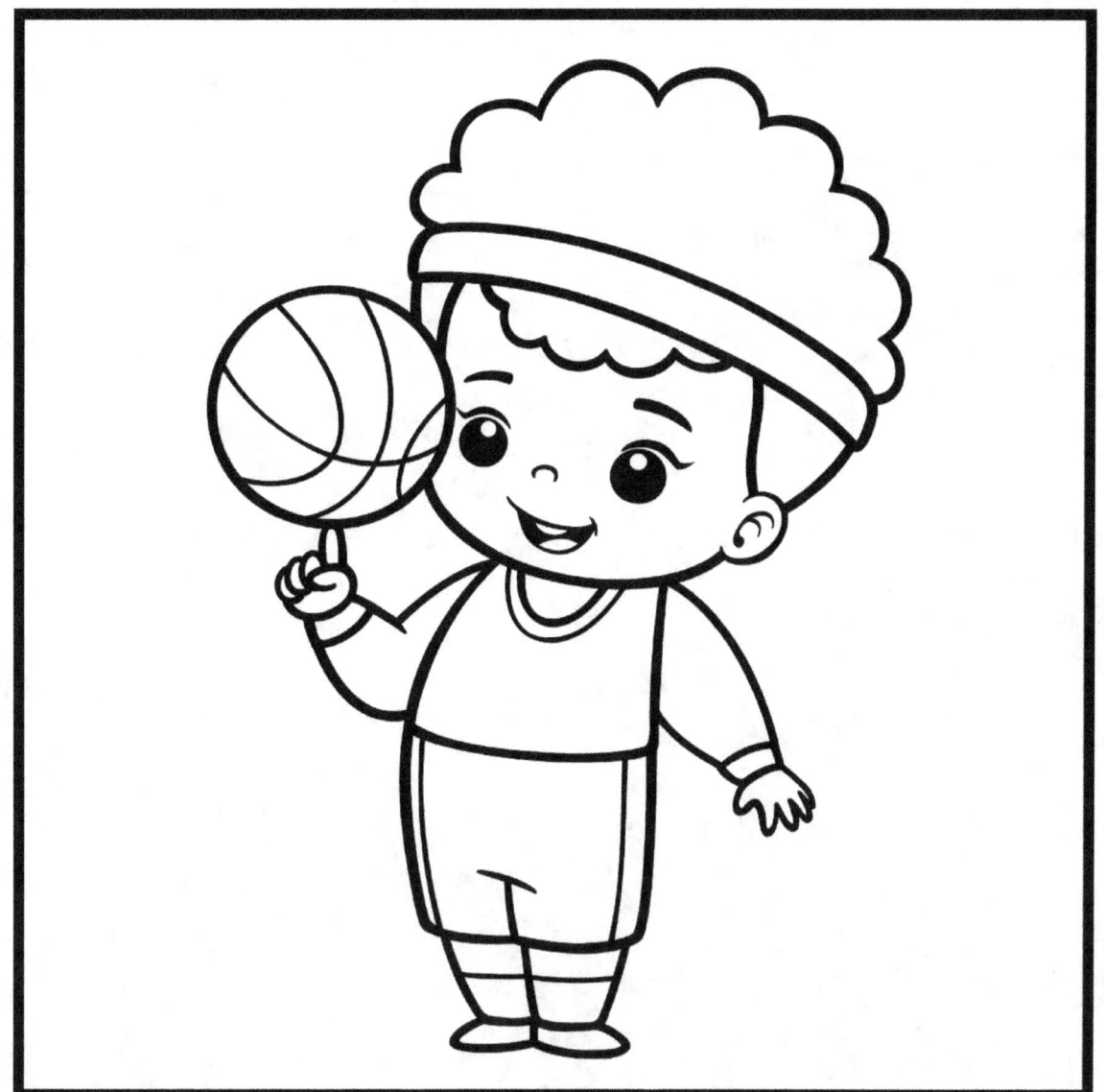

note:

_____

_____

_____

NOVEMBER 34TH

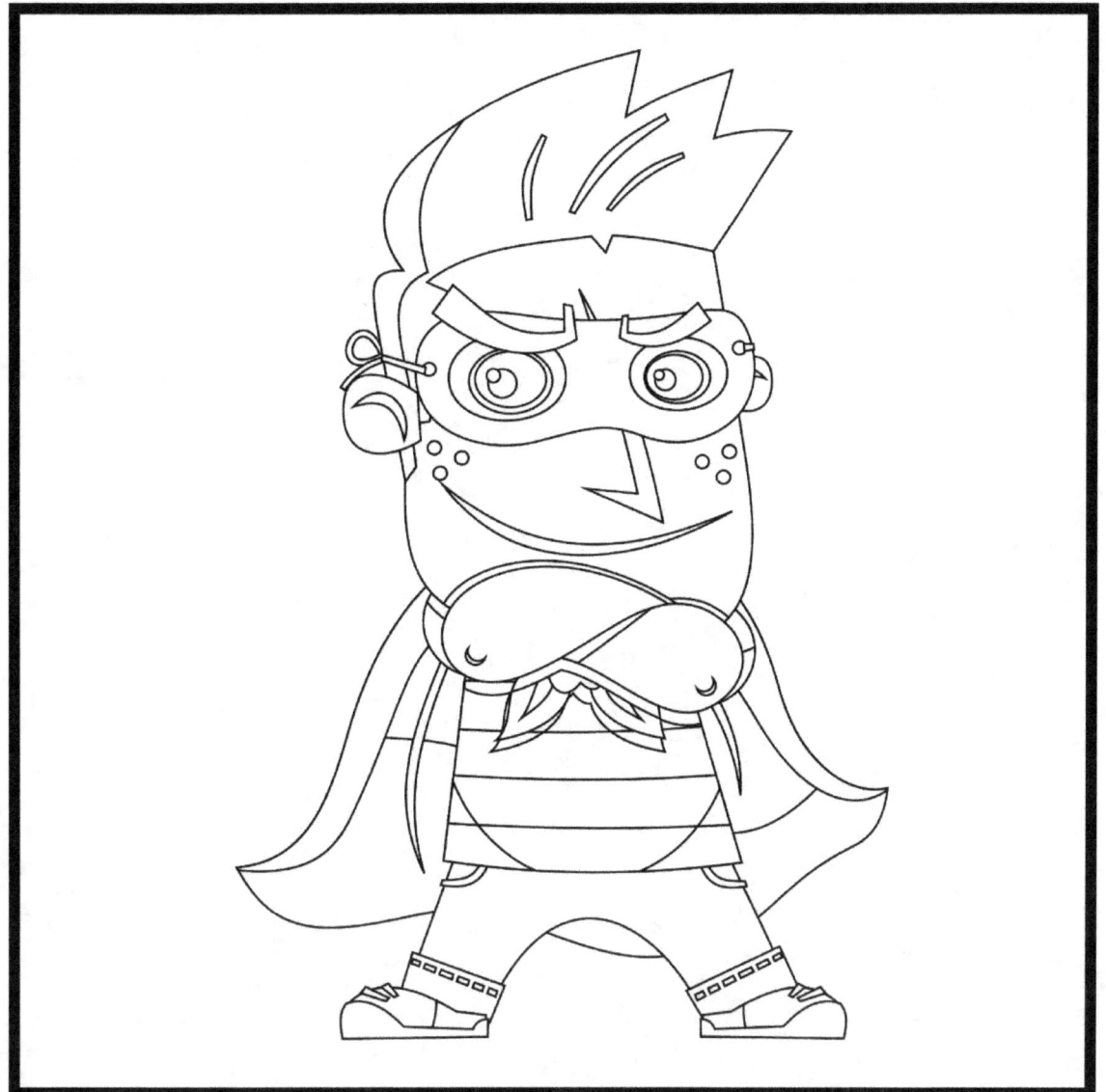

note:

_____

_____

_____

NOVEMBER 35TH

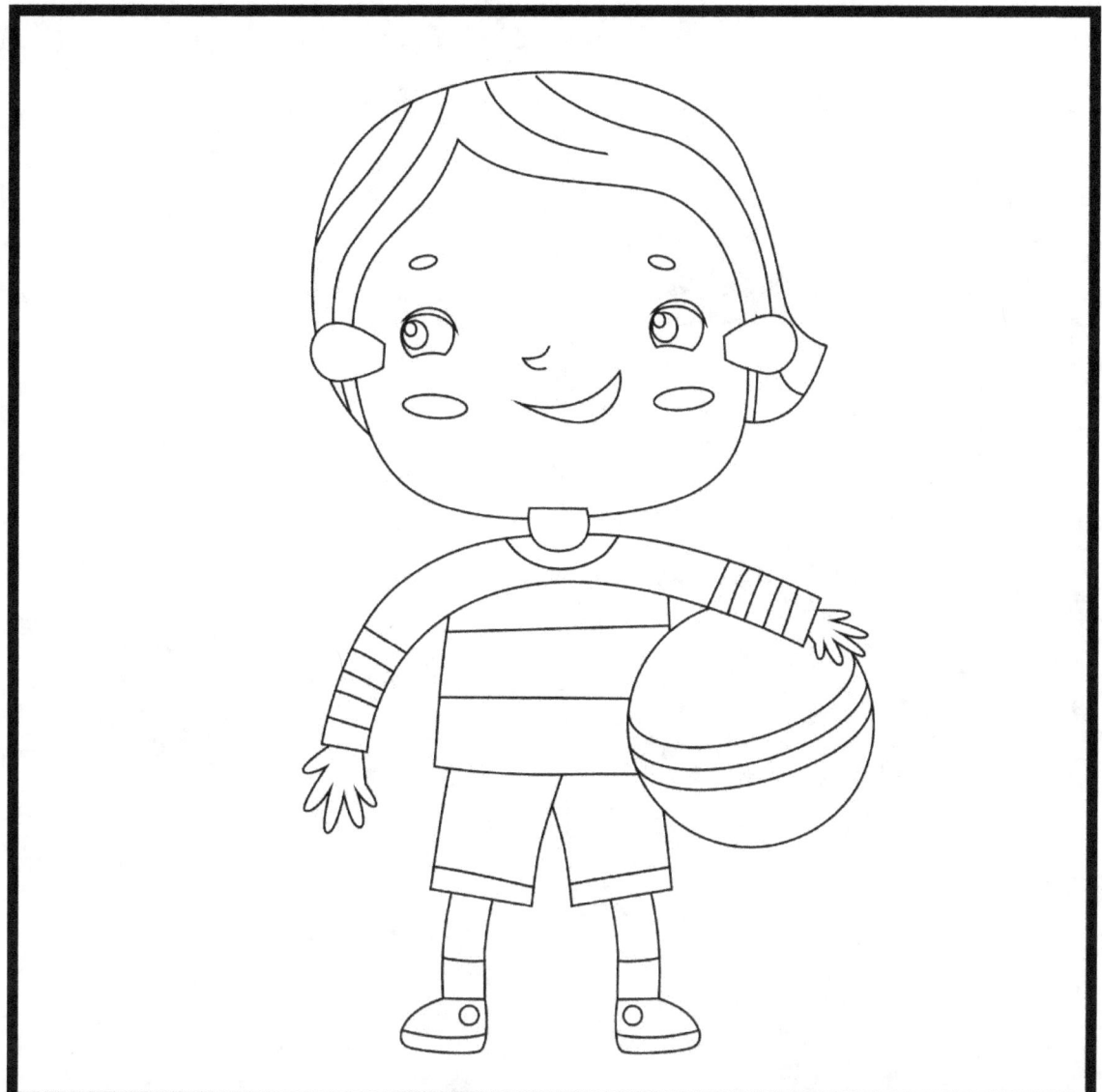

note:

_____

_____

_____

NOVEMBER 36TH

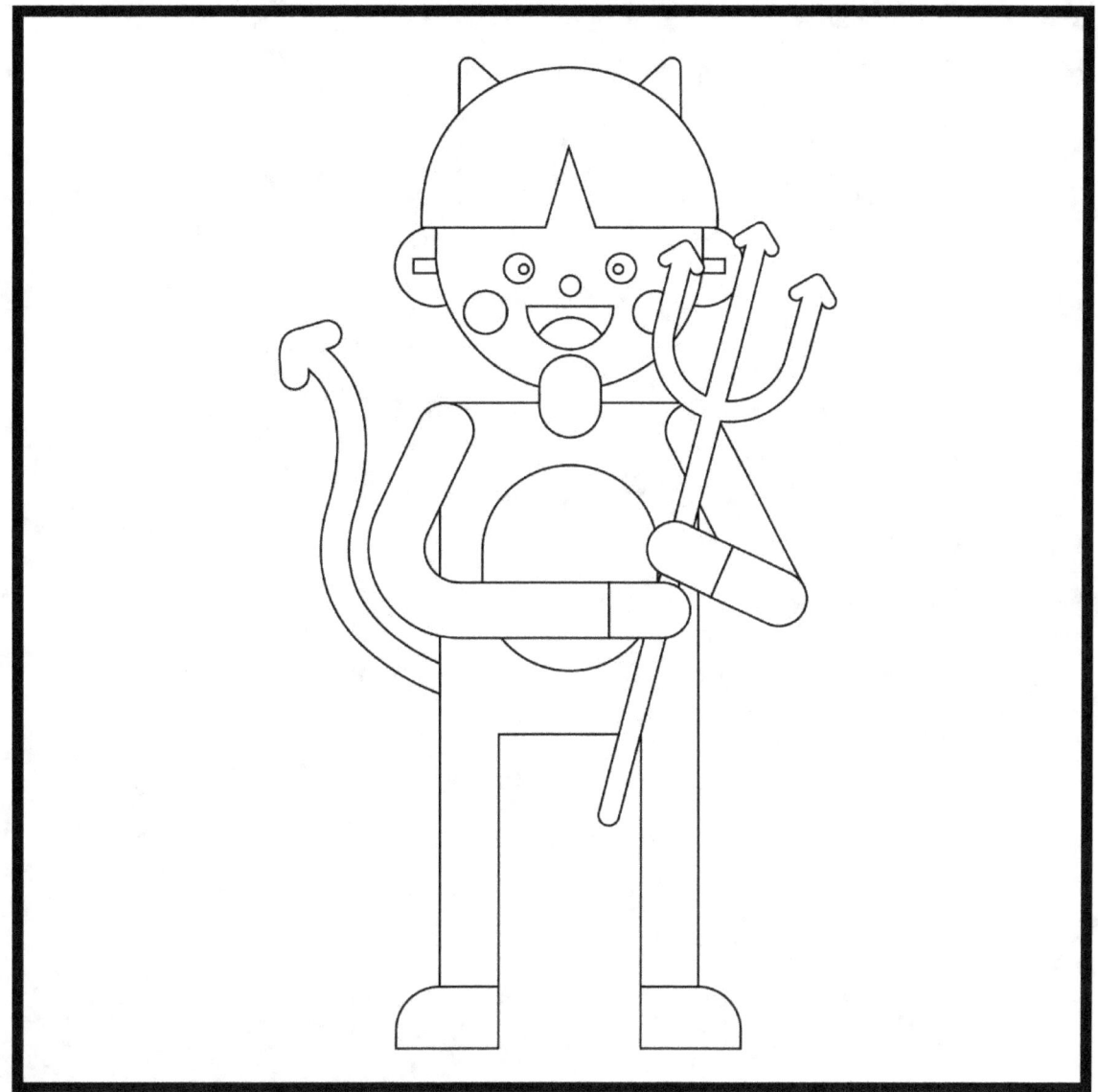

note:

_____

_____

_____

NOVEMBER 37TH

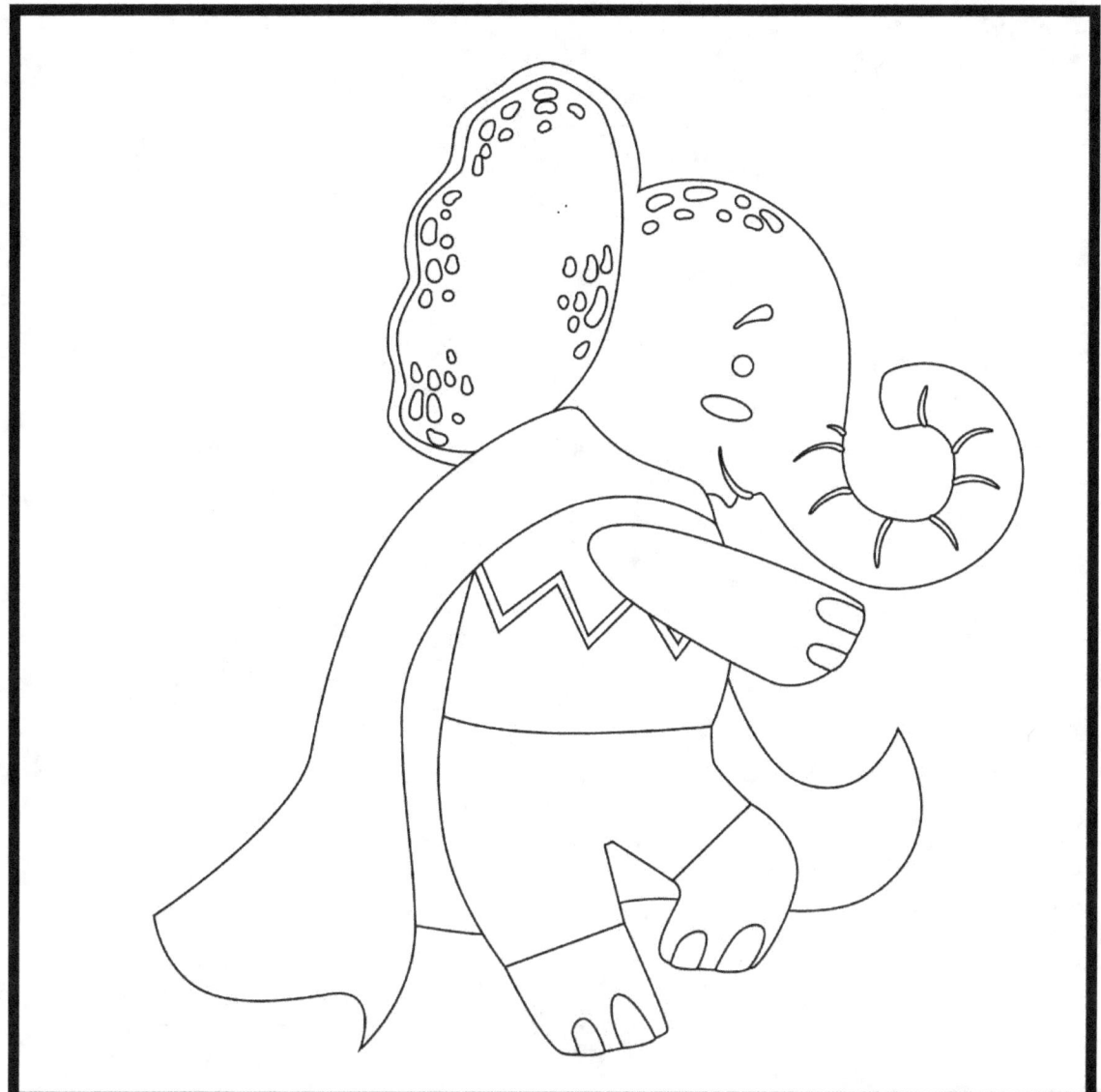

note:

_____

_____

_____

NOVEMBER 38TH

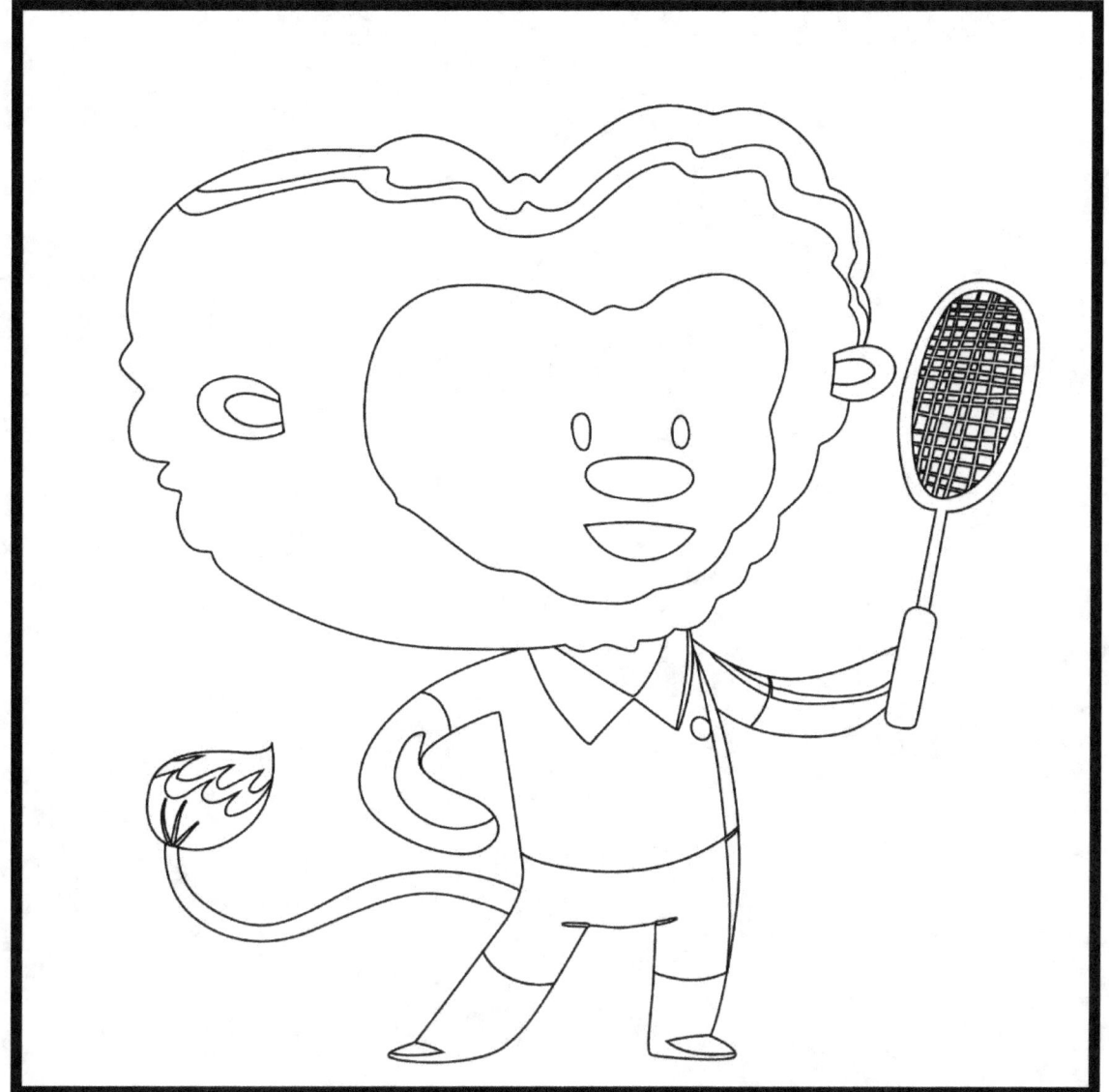

note:

_____

_____

_____

NOVEMBER 39TH

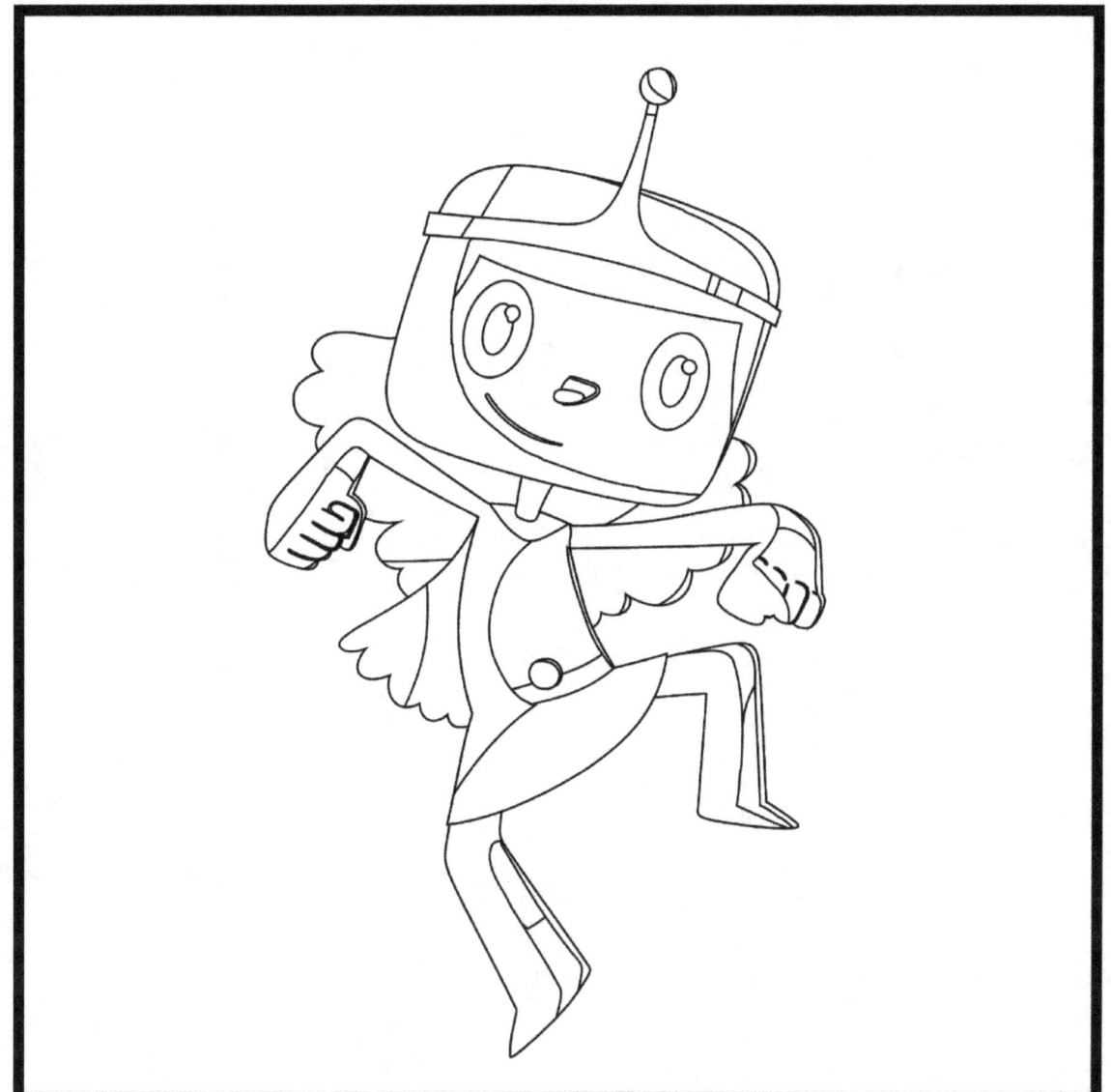

note:

_____

_____

_____

NOVEMBER 40TH

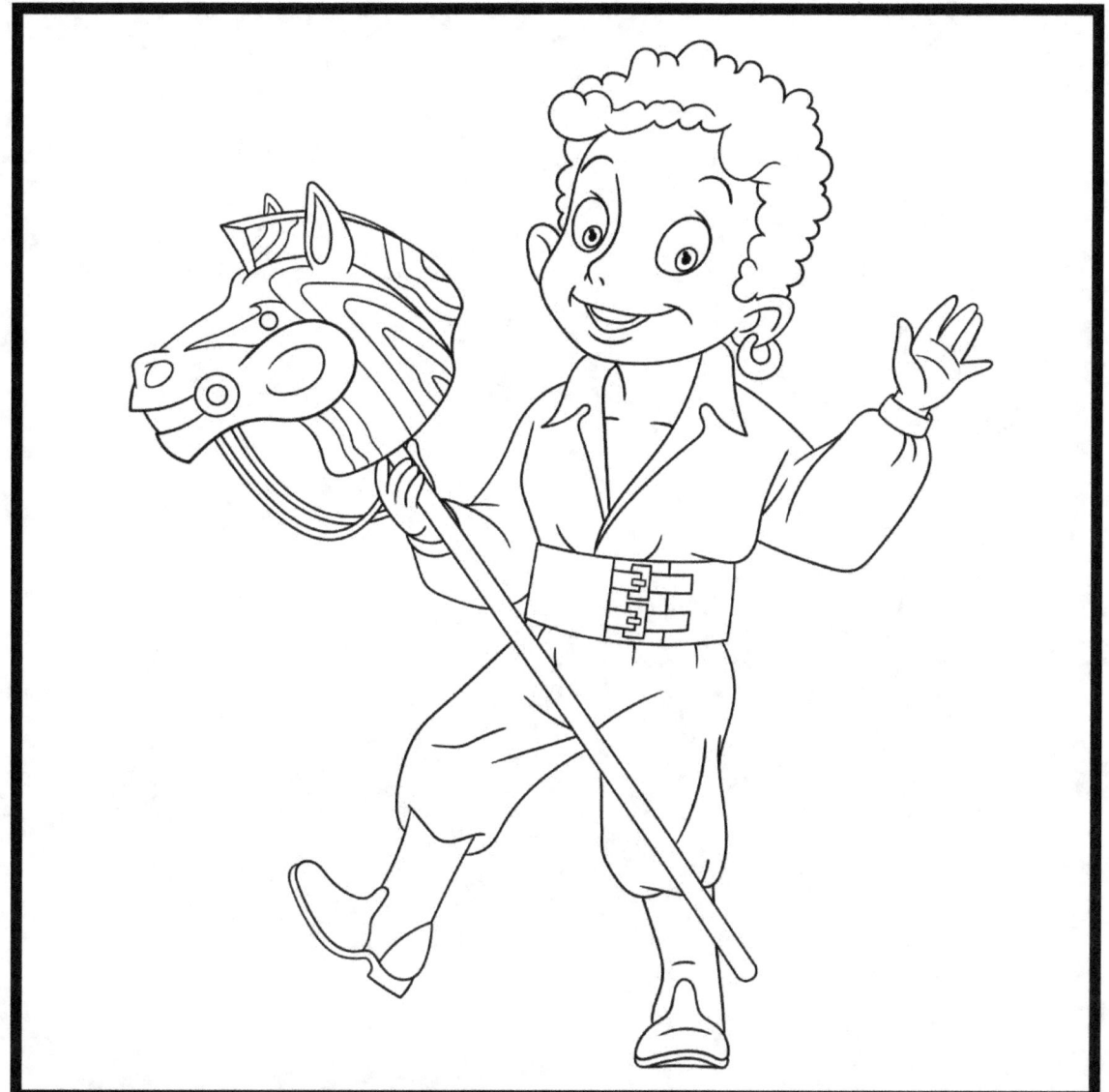

note:

_____

_____

_____

NOVEMBER 41TH

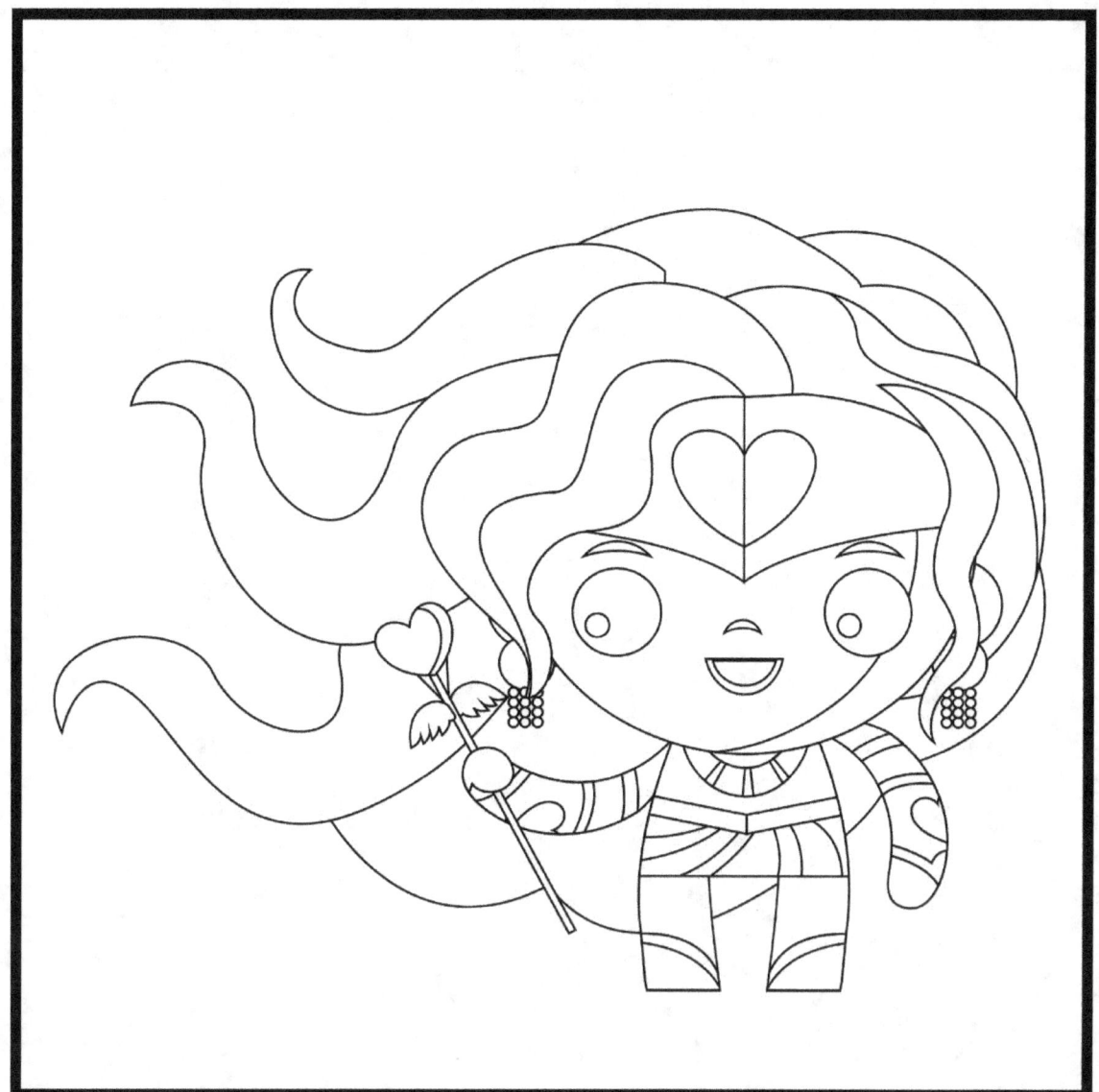

note:

_____

_____

_____

NOVEMBER 42TH

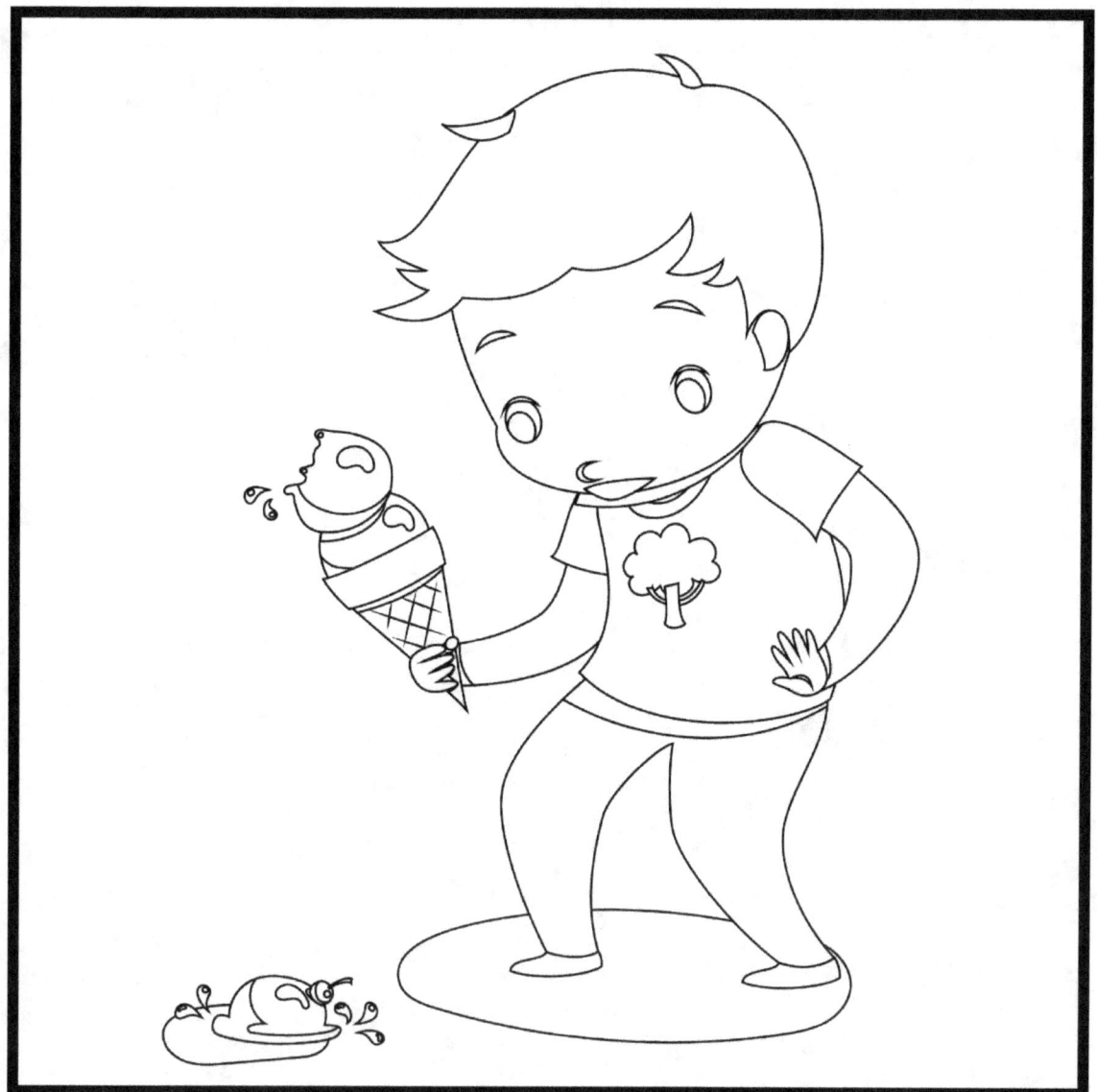

note:

_____

_____

_____

NOVEMBER 43TH

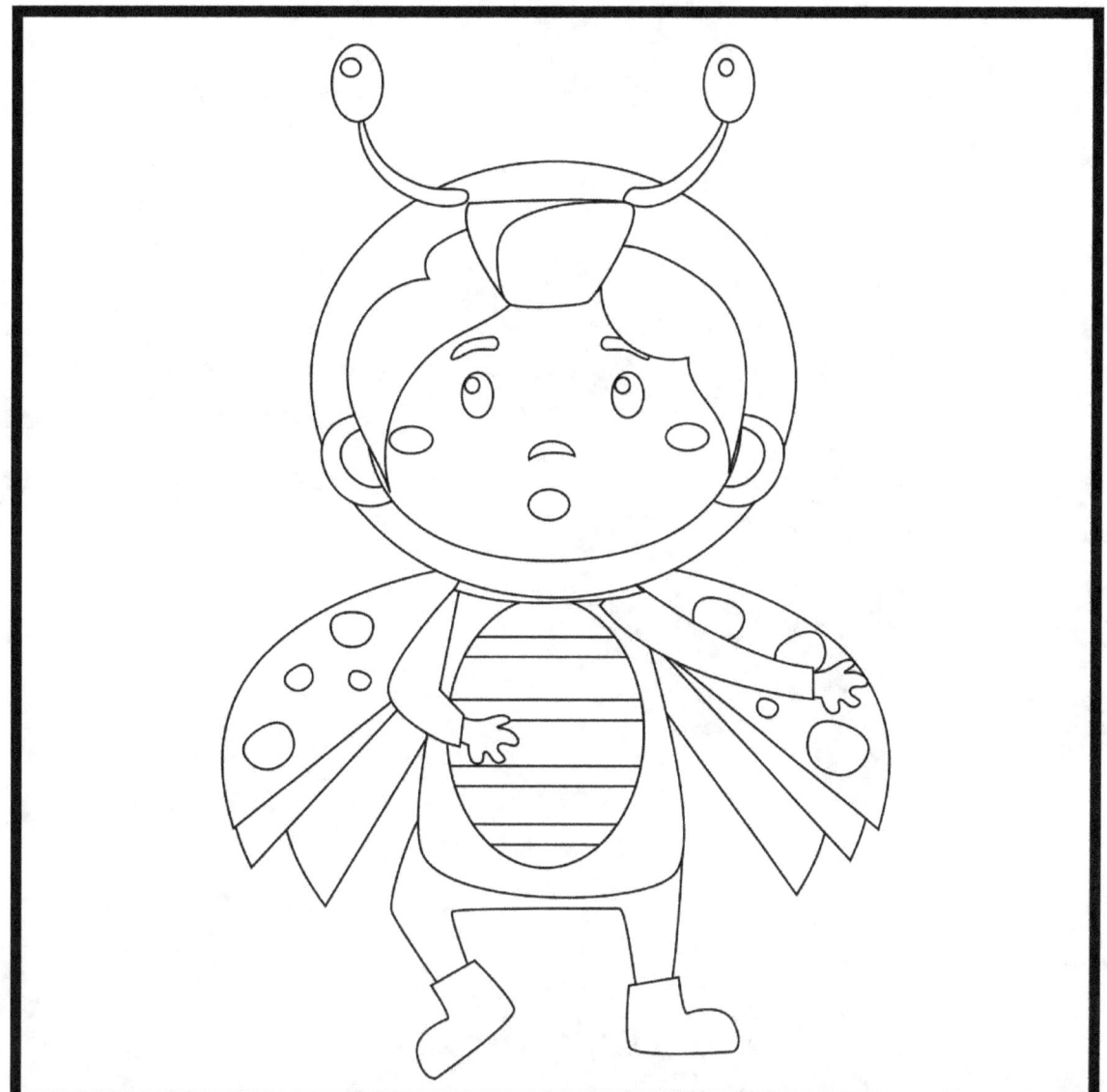

note:

_____

_____

_____

NOVEMBER 44TH

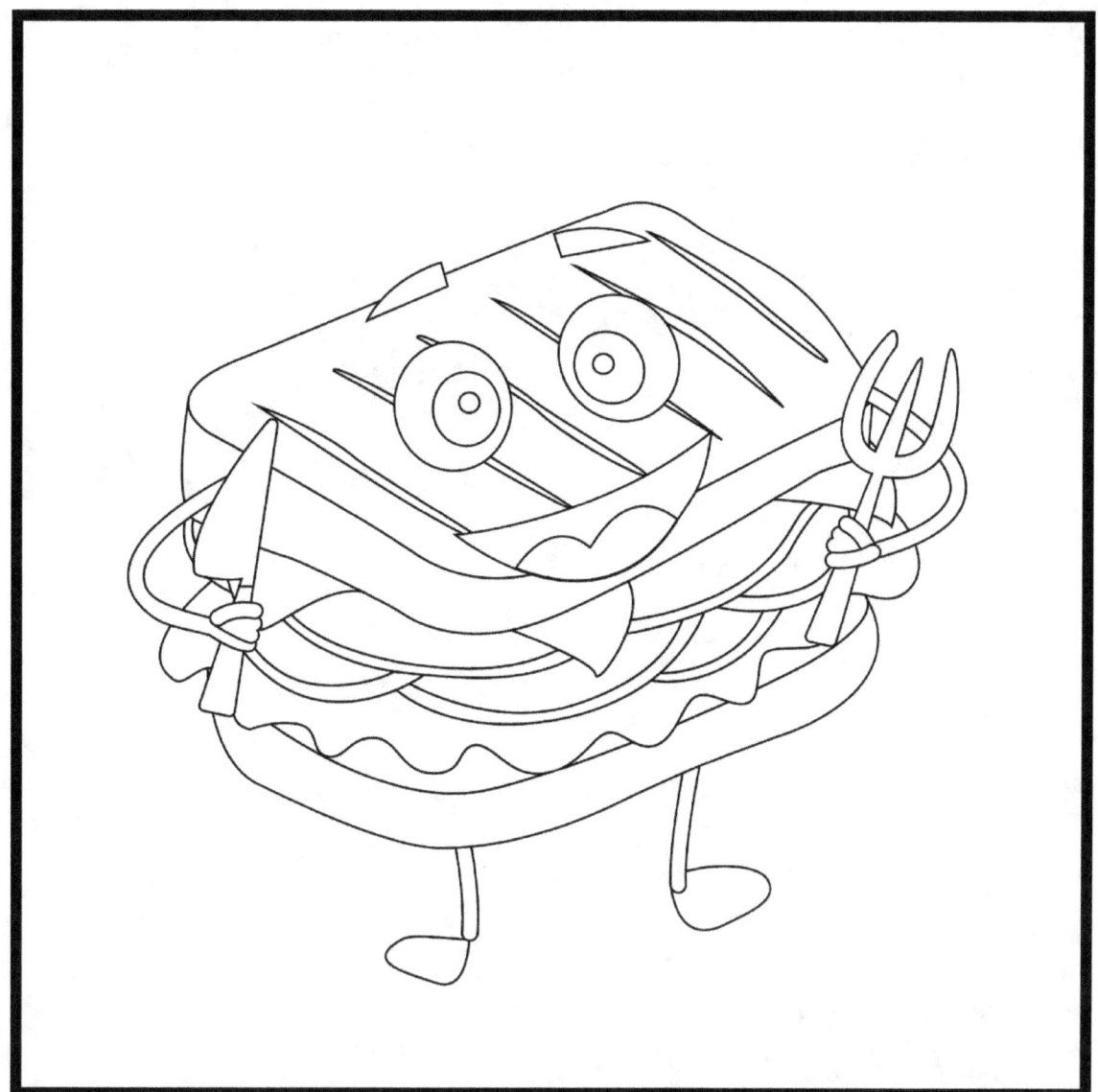

note:

_____

_____

_____

NOVEMBER 45TH

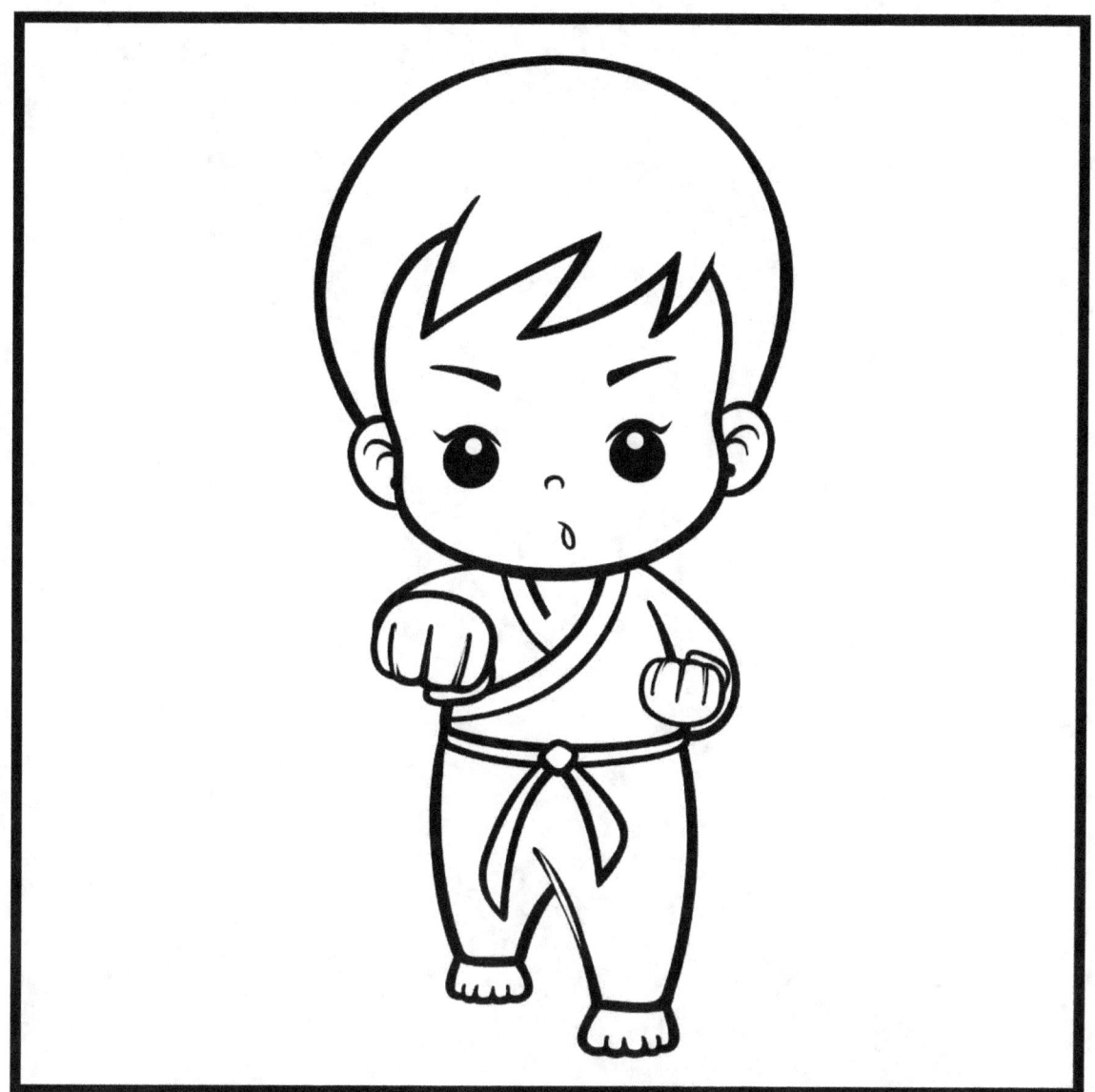

note:

_____

_____

_____

NOVEMBER 46TH

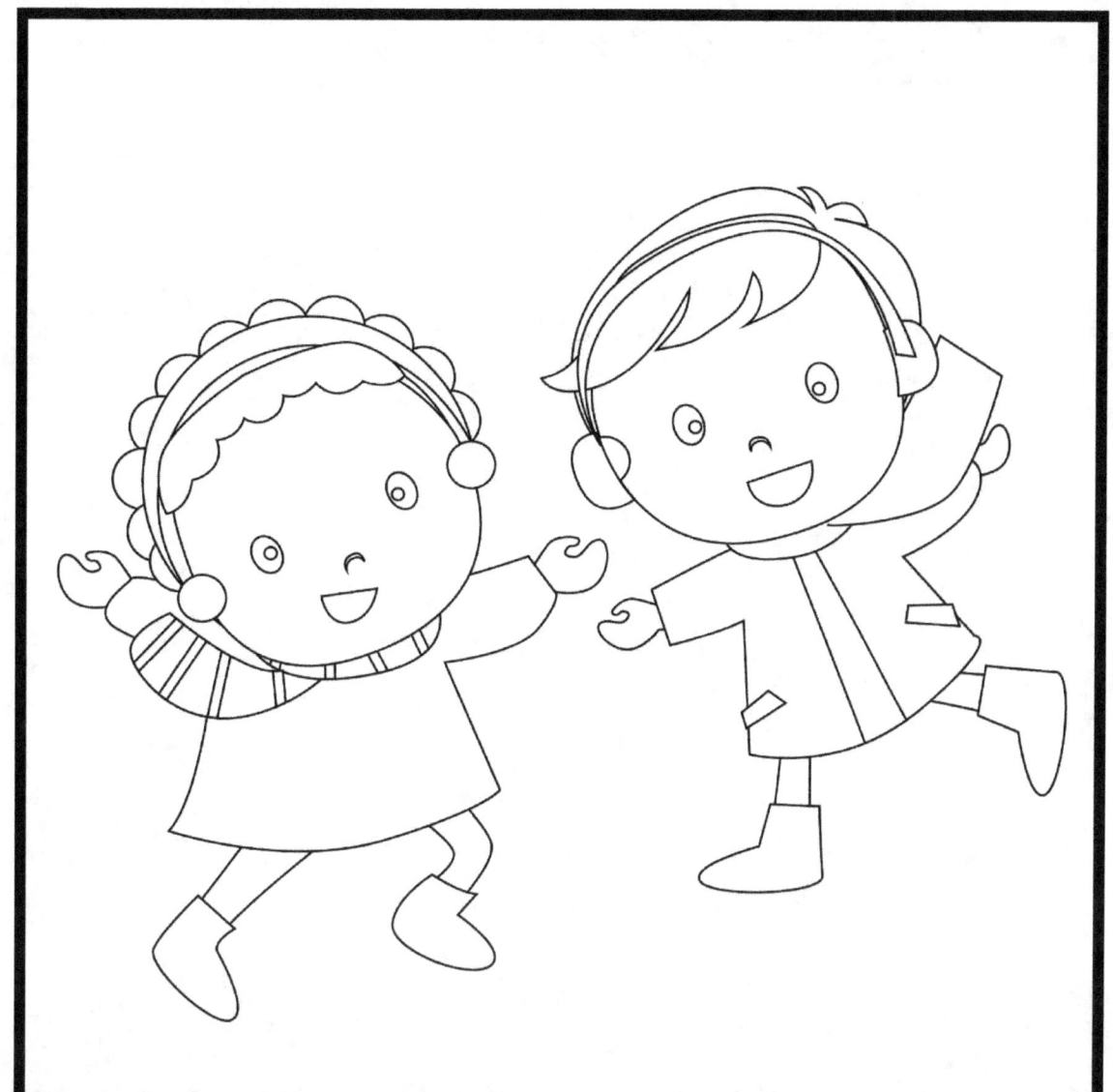

note:

_____

_____

_____

NOVEMBER 47TH

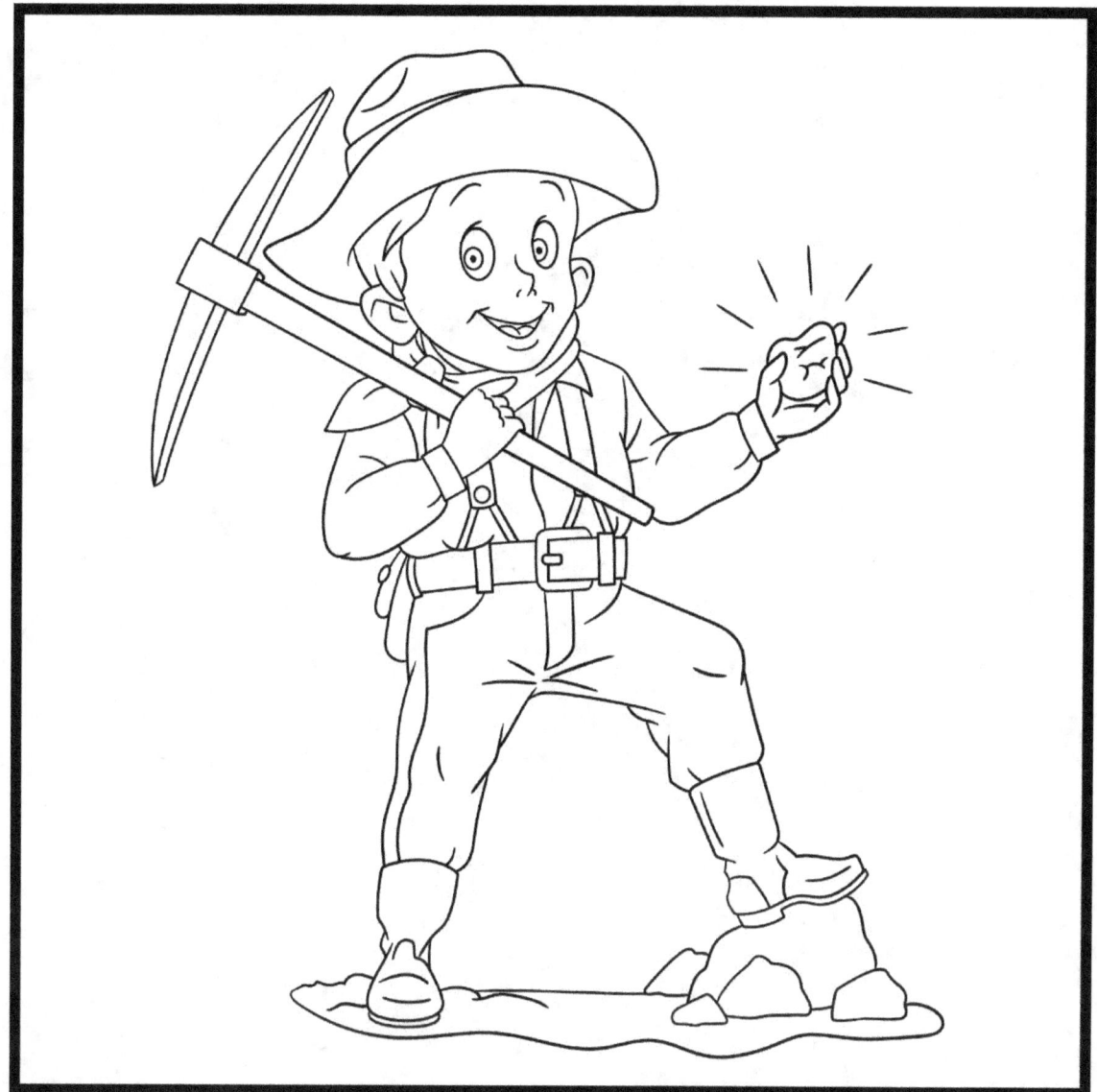

note:

_____

_____

_____

NOVEMBER 48TH

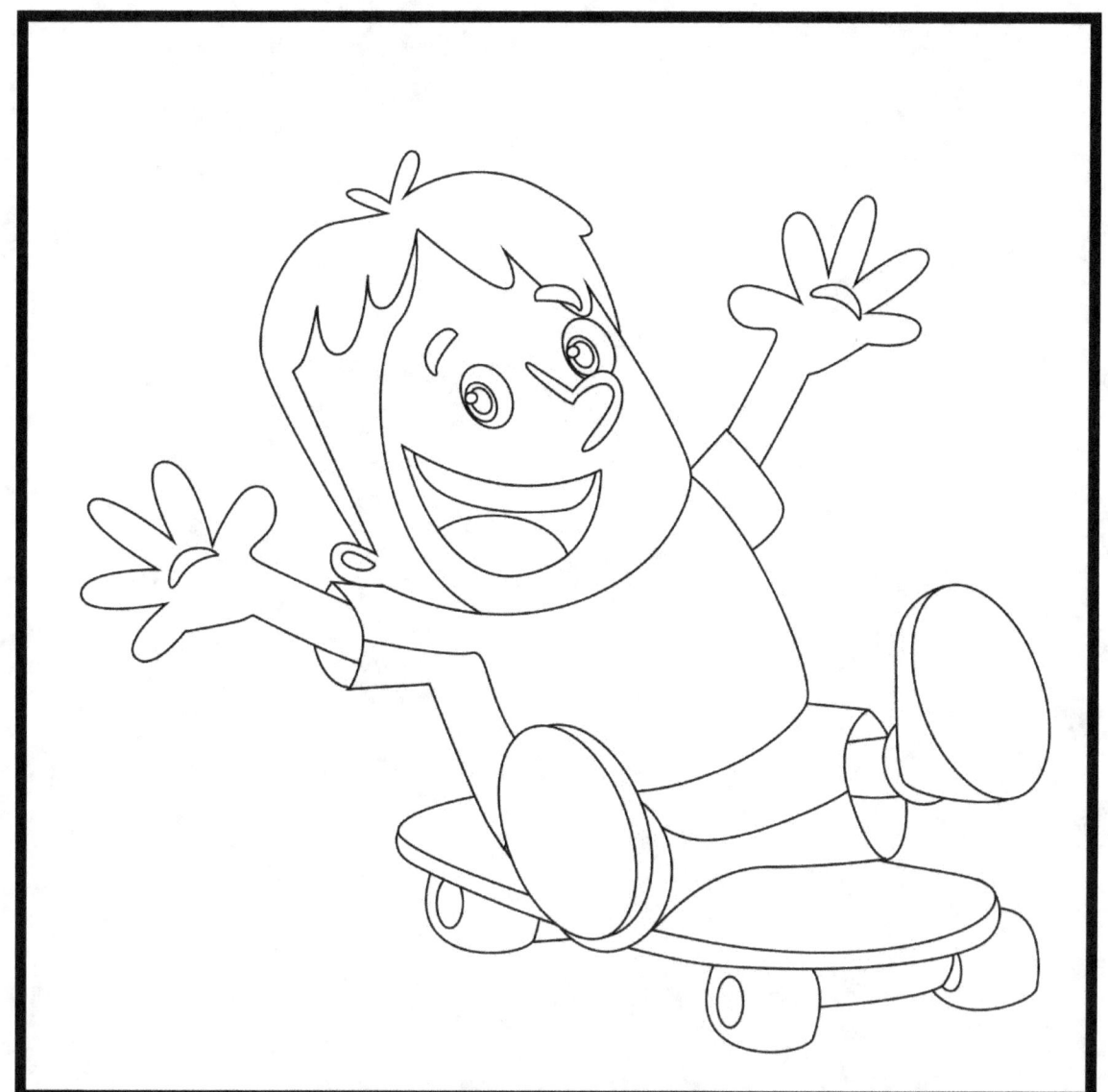

note:

_____

_____

_____

NOVEMBER 49TH

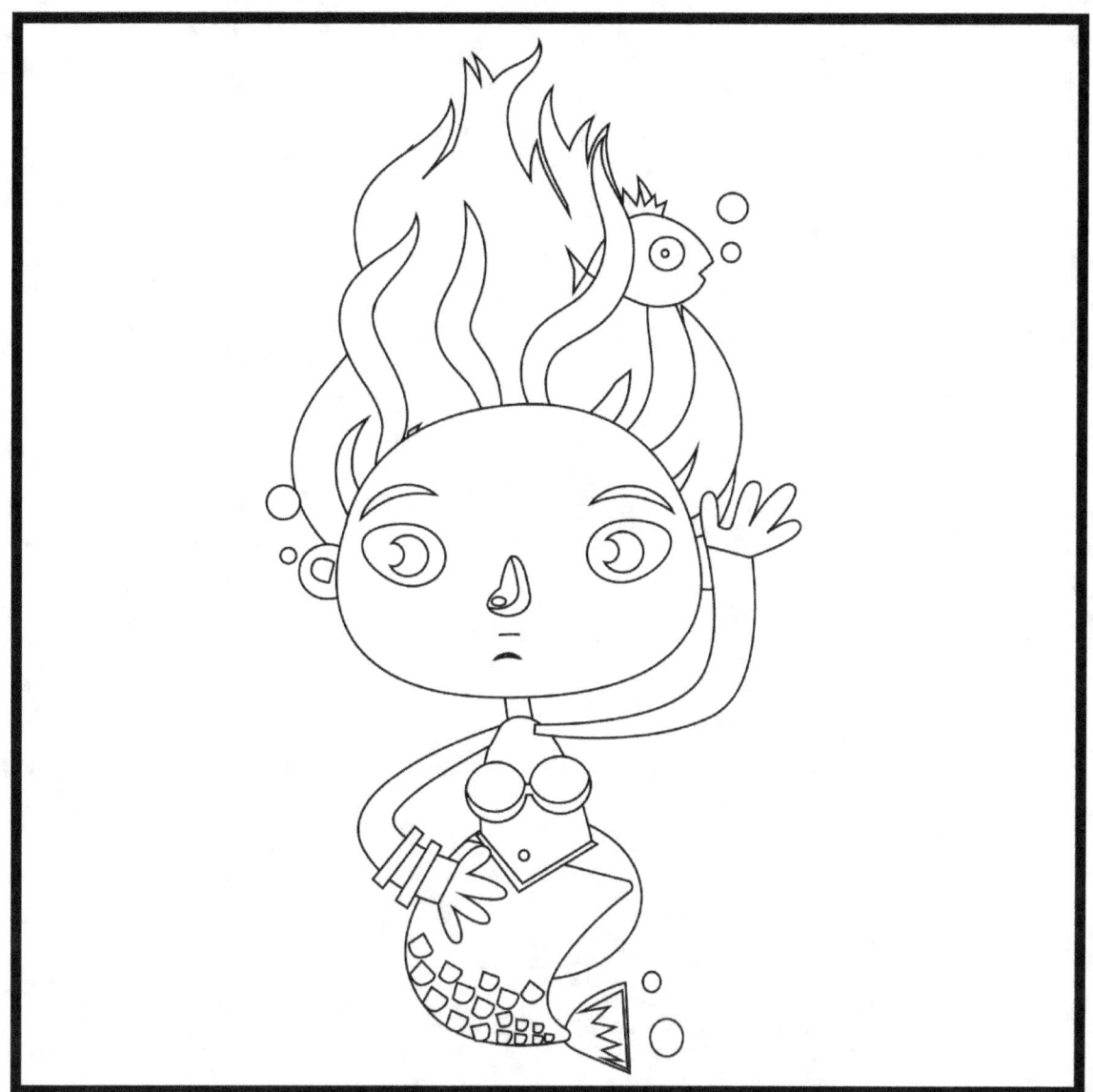

note:

_____

_____

_____

NOVEMBER 50TH

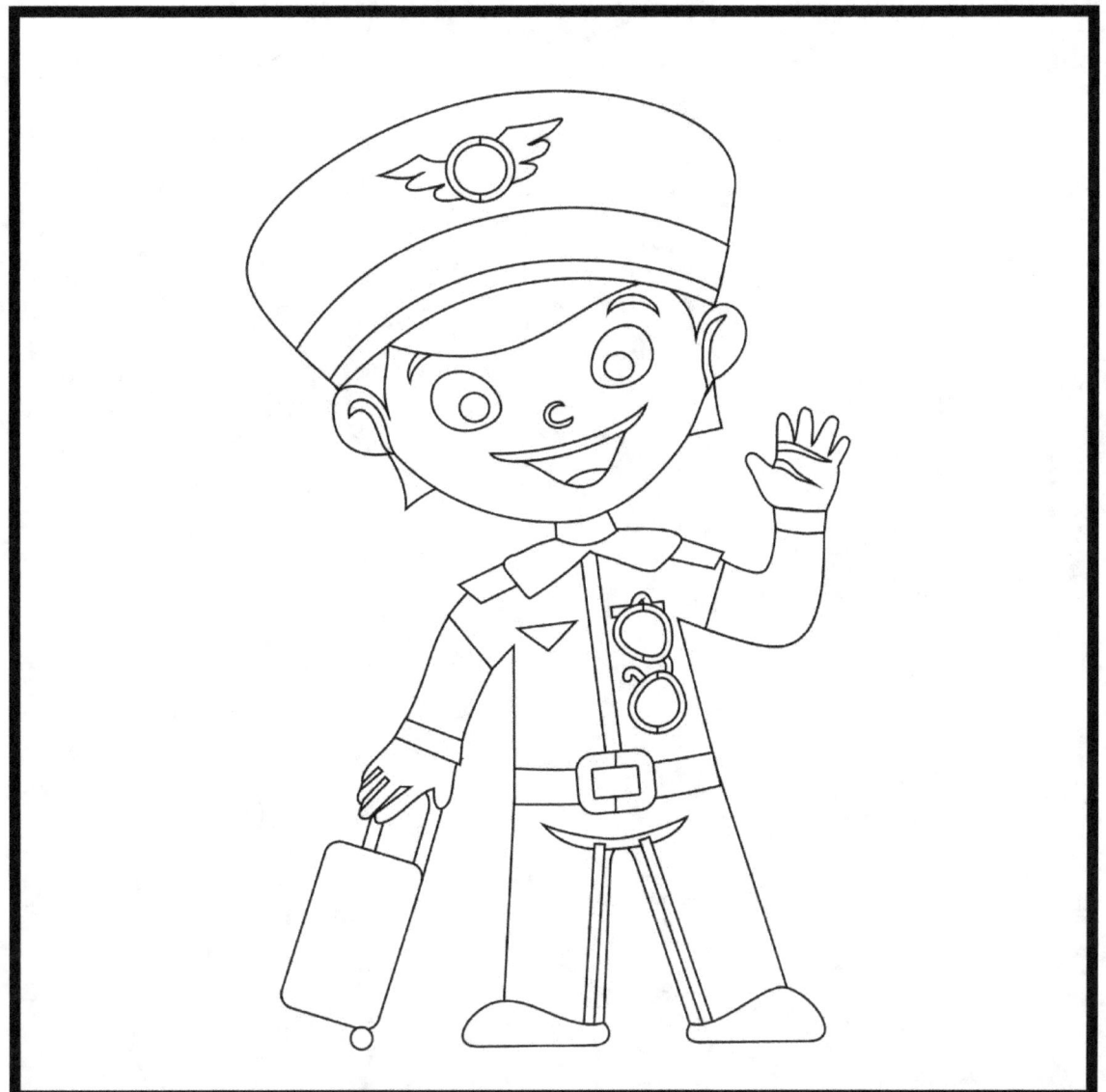

note:

_____

_____

_____